Praise for *Make It in America*

"If you want to do business in the United States, *Make It in America* should be at the top of your reading list. Every entrepreneur and business leader will benefit from Matthew Lee Sawyer's valuable strategic insights, relevant case studies, and useful tools to develop your own playbook for success."

—**Dorie Clark**, *Wall Street Journal* bestselling author of *The Long Game* and executive education faculty at Duke University Fuqua School of Business

"Matthew Lee Sawyer offers thoughtful advice for any businessperson looking to market and build their business in the United States. In this book he offers specific examples and a commonsense approach to tackling the ever-changing U.S. marketplace. This book could be titled *Start Here*, and you'd be wise to do so."

—**Beth Comstock**, author of *Imagine It Forward* and former vice chair of GE

"Matthew Lee Sawyer provides the perfect how-to-guide for anyone wanting to pursue the American Dream in business. He combines his expert strategic sense from academia with his passion for global citizens to enable the next chapter in the entrepreneurially melting pot that has America what it is today. Prospective and current business leaders both would be well-served to read and absorb every bit of his well-researched advice."

—**Ray Day**, vice chair at Stagwell (and former chief communications officer at Ford and IBM)

"Through great examples, clear frameworks, and tangible, practical recommendations, Matthew Sawyer demystifies the complexities of entering the U.S. market. He directly addresses the challenges of generalizing about the U.S. consumer, thinking you can do it alone, and many other assumptions that you'll have to toss aside if you are serious about making it in America. And he does it with a friendly, easy-to-follow tone that simplifies the technical and keeps your eyes on what is important.

A great guidebook that you'll just keep referring to throughout your U.S.-bound business journey."

—**David Edelman**, Harvard Business School professor, former AETNA chief marketing officer, and McKinsey partner

"The United States has long been a beacon for the world's entrepreneurs. Given the relatively short history of the country, every global giant that has been founded in the United States was formed by a first- through fourth-generation immigrant! What makes America fundamentally different from much of the rest of the world—both developed and emerging—are its clear rule of law, the near total absence of endemic corruption, and its pro-business laws and government. And that is before one even considers the market size, partnership opportunities, and availability of skilled cofounders and employees.

Matthew Lee Sawyer's *Make It in America* is an introduction to starting a business written specifically for international founders and businesses. It clearly lays out the benefits and challenges of beginning your business in—or transferring it to—the United States. This book should be mandatory reading for anyone considering bringing their entrepreneurial dream to the United States."

—**David S. Rose**, founder of Gust and the New York Angels and founding general partner of True Global Ventures

"'Culture eats strategy for breakfast' is a famous saying that every entrepreneur should take to heart, especially when going abroad. Setting up a venture overseas costs time and money. Going in blind is a sure way to waste hundreds of thousands of dollars. Matthew's book is a cookbook helping to ensure a perfect landing into the United States. Short, concise, yet complete, it offers readers hands-on advice to make it in the United States and get a better understanding of its cultural intricacies and ways of building a successful business in the United States. Together with our Country Comparison, Matthew's book is a must-read for anybody wanting to create an American dream."

—**Egbert Schram**, group CEO at Hofstede Insights

"The biggest mistake companies make when entering the U.S. market is focusing too much on products and services. It's much more important to get the culture and marketing aspects right so you effectively appeal to discerning buyers. In *Make It in America*, Matthew Lee Sawyer shows you how."

—**David Meerman Scott**, international bestselling author of *The New Rules of Marketing and PR*

"Matthew Lee Sawyer combines deep strategic and marketing experience, decades of professional competence in U.S. and global markets, natural curiosity and the will to dig deeper into any topic, an academic's eye for bigger picture understanding and practical skill development, the consultant's desire to diverge and converge to solve and move forward, empathy, and genuine kindness and care to suggest a strategic framework and implementation roadmap to launch into and grow in the U.S. market.

"Simply said, anyone dreaming to come to the United States, regardless of the industry and business idea, will benefit from *Make It in America*. If you want to succeed, read from the master! I learn with every interaction I have with Matthew, and his book is an awesome extension of that!"

—**Marc Somnolet**, president of the French-American Chamber of Commerce and former worldwide director of global marketing at Colgate Palmolive

"Entrepreneurship has always been difficult, but doing it in a foreign country is even more so. Besides the typical business barriers and lack of networks, language and cultural hurdles hinder the road to success. Foreign startups need support and a roadmap, and this book gives concrete tools to understand the American culture and basic concepts of doing business in the United States.

"I recommend this book to conscious entrepreneurs looking for guidance and hoping to enter the U.S. market as their next big step."

—**Fernanda Soza**, executive director at Chile Massachusetts Alliance

"As an entrepreneur from Pakistan who has launched three ventures in the United States, I've encountered many challenges here. This book is a solid and valuable guide for overseas entrepreneurs seeking to enter the lucrative American market."

—**Nasir Wajihuddin**, founder and CEO of Anedom Mobile Group

"Matthew Lee Sawyer's book is a must-read for anyone who wants to expand their business into the United States. As an immigration lawyer, I send my clients to several places to research how to start their companies in the United States, so their immigration visa applications will be successful. This book is a one-stop shop for learning all the steps a company must consider and act on to succeed in their business ventures in America."

—**Tahmina Watson**, founder of Watson Immigration Law and author of *The Startup Visa*

MAKE IT =IN= AMERICA★

MAKE IT =IN= AMERICA★

How International Companies and Entrepreneurs Can Successfully Enter and Scale in U.S. Markets

MATTHEW LEE SAWYER

WILEY

Published by John Wiley & Sons, Inc., Hoboken, New Jersey.
Published simultaneously in Canada.

For general information on our other products and services or for technical support, please contact our Customer Care Department within the United States at (800) 762-2974, outside the United States at (317) 572-3993 or fax (317) 572-4002.

Wiley publishes in a variety of print and electronic formats and by print-on-demand. Some material included with standard print versions of this book may not be included in e-books or in print-on-demand. If this book refers to media such as a CD or DVD that is not included in the version you purchased, you may download this material at http://booksupport.wiley.com. For more information about Wiley products, visit www.wiley.com.

Library of Congress Cataloging-in-Publication Data:

Names: Sawyer, Matthew Lee, author.
Title: Make it in America : how international companies and entrepreneurs can successfully enter and scale in U.S. markets / Matthew Lee Sawyer.
Description: Hoboken, New Jersey : Wiley, [2022] | Includes index.
Identifiers: LCCN 2022033483 (print) | LCCN 2022033482 (ebook) | ISBN 9781119885146 (hardback) | ISBN 9781119885160 (adobe pdf) | ISBN 9781119885153 (epub)
Subjects: LCSH: Corporations, Foreign—United States. | International business enterprises—United States.
Classification: LCC HD2785 .S38 2022 (ebook) | LCC HD2785 (print) | DDC 338.8/88973 23/eng/20220—dc21
LC record available at https://urldefense.com/v3/__https://lccn.loc.gov/2022033483

Cover Design: Peter L. Levine
Cover Image: © mockups-design.com
Author photo: © Peter Serling, 2022

SKY10036523_101822

Dedicated to Helen and Bob Sawyer who gave me the encouragement, love, and support to pursue my American Dream.

Contents

Acknowledgments

This book would not have happened without the help of many people. With the risk of forgetting to mention a few, I want to acknowledge those who were especially helpful.

For sharing their expert knowledge of international business and connections: Josh Berliner of Israeli Economic Mission; Jabril Brisendine at Triana Group; Gemma Cortijo at Spain-U.S. Chamber of Commerce; Irene Fuchs and Dietmar Rieg of German American Chamber of Commerce; Ian Houston at Scottish Business Network; Joacim Mattisson at Swedish-American Chamber of Commerce; Francisco Samper at MullenLowe Latin America; Fernanda Soza and Beatriz Valdivia at ChileMass; Federico Tozzi at Italy-America Chamber of Commerce; and Valerie Van den Keybus at BelCham.

For help finding industry data and research: Tosin Agbabbiak at Octopus Ventures; Justin Kreamer at New York City Economic Development Corporation; Walter Charnizon at TechDay HQ; Patrick Santillo at Business Council for International Understanding; Giulia Imperatrice, Frances Simowitz, and Shai Tamary at WEVE Acceleration.

For insights about cultural factors: Sefanit Befekadu at CVS Health, Christine Straw at Columbia University; Lisa Bevill at IE University; Lisa DeWaard, Martin Karaffa, and Egbert Schram at Hofstede Insights; Doug Quackenbos at University of South Carolina; Michael Stallard at Connecting Culture Group; and Duke Urbanik at Masters of Scale.

For the chapter on legal and tax considerations: Daniel Glazer at Wilson Sonsini Goodrich & Rosati's U.S. Expansion group and London office; Randy Heller at Gallet Dryer & Berkey; Jake Heyka of King & Spalding; Scott Smedresman at Brown Rudnick; Martin Vorbrodt at Fredricks & von der Horst; and Steven Zelson at Pursuit Intellectual Property Consulting.

For information about U.S. immigration and visas: Marko Issever at America EB5 Visa; Zoia Kozakov of Women in Innovation; Barbara McGloin at Columbia University; and Tahmina Watson at Watson Immigration Law.

For information about issues surrounding employment and community: Alain Charbonnier of MyExPat.US; Alice Chin at Your Other Half; Antoine Guillaud and Leentje De Leeuw at International Management Solutions; Doug Gross at NG Data; Waichiro Hayashi at Hayashi Ventures; Bill Kenney at Soft Land Partners; Bob Kobayashi at Odgers Berndtson; Paul Reed at ADP; and Suzanne Southard at Swedish Women's Educational Association International.

For help with the chapter on financing and capital structure: J. Skyler "Sky" Fernandes at VU Venture Partners; Xavier Lederer at Ambrose; Julie Morrison at Scottish Enterprise; David S. Rose at Gust, New York Angels, and True Global Ventures; Thomas Løgstrup Riebs at AXEL; Neil Schwartzreich at MullenLowe; Andy Tsao and Michael Zuckert at Silicon Valley Bank.

For insights and information on marketing: Olivia Butter at Klarna; Kevin Coupe at Morning News Beat; David Edelman at Harvard Business School; Rob Goldberg at Broadridge; David Polinchok at Brand Experience Lab; Jim Licenski at Northwestern University; Ole Pedersen at Droga5; Marc Somnolet at the French-American Chamber of Commerce and NYU; Patrick Spear at GMDC; and Kai Wright at Columbia University.

For letting me interview them and tell their stories: Chris and Natasha Ashton of Petplan; Bruce Buchanan and Pascal Ehrsam at Rokt; John Affel and David Burrows at World Finer Foods; Dino Borri and Sara Massarotto at Eataly; Christian Chemaly at Polar Stock; Matthias Farwick at Txture; Pierre Gervois at Legit Productions; Juan Pablo Gnecco of MediaCom; MaryAnne Howland and Tobias Reisman at HDTI; Julián Jaramillo of Alpina Foods; Jason Riback at MediaMint; Sophia "Puff" Story at 3 Sided Cube; Silvia Vanni at ShareMyBag; Gilles Vanpouke at Renson; and Scott Weir at Pillow Partners.

For support and guidance on writing and editing: Dorie Clark; Tom Cotton, Lucy McCauley; Thomas Mellins, Randy Milgrom, J.D. Schram, and Jonathan Towers.

For creating the terrific design work: Peter Levine, art director; Andrew Sawyer, digital designer; and Peter Serling, photographer.

To the team at Wiley Publishing: Michelle Hacker, Matt Kissner, Jozette Moses; Zachary Schisgel, Shannon Vargo, and Kim Wimpsett. And to my lawyer: Ken Weinrib at Franklin, Weinrib, Rudell & Vassallo.

Finally, and most deserving of acknowledgment, I want to thank my wife, Sharon. She gave me the encouragement and support to be able to devote 18 months to this project.

Introduction

All my life, I've heard about the American Dream. In fact, I'm a product of it. My ancestors emigrated from Eastern Europe in the early 1900s. When they got to the United States, they struggled to find menial jobs and start families. My grandfather, Louis Needleman, joked about wearing plaid pants made from his sister's dresses until he went into the Army.

Later Louis worked as a traveling salesperson, but eventually he and his wife, Tillie, moved to Newport, Vermont, near the Canadian border and opened their own business: the American Clothing Company. They did so well that soon they moved to a bigger location in a newly constructed block of buildings. Eventually, Louis was able to buy the whole block, and he also became a director at the local bank.

Louis became a good citizen, too, sharing what he had and what he'd learned with the people around him. When he died in 1964, his obituary in the local newspaper read: "He was always interested in the betterment of the community in which he and his family made their home. Many of his kindnesses and thoughtful deeds have not been known as he chose to do good for its sake alone and not for personal praise."[1]

Louis Needleman's success had far exceeded anything his parents had imagined when they landed in the United States, and his life has served as an inspiration to his descendants, including me. It seemed only fitting, then, that I write a book that might help other people achieve their American Dream.

If you're an executive or entrepreneur who wishes to bring your business into the United States, *Make It in America* will show you how to profitably enter and scale your company on our shores. Additionally, this book is also useful for Americans who are working with international businesspeople. It will help you create fruitful alliances by making you more aware of the challenges and issues that non-U.S. nationals face.

Make It in America is not a "How To" manual in the conventional sense. Although there are several strategic frameworks and checklists, there are no recipes or instructions. Rather, this book provides an overview of the practices, external factors, and cultural characteristics found across the U.S. business landscape, including explanations on how and why they developed. Each chapter focuses on a question that international entrepreneurs have asked me that they considered most critical for their business journey. There are sections that introduce legal, financing, managing people, and visa issues, as well as lessons from international companies to help you identify potential difficulties and pitfalls.

At the end of each chapter, you will find case study examples that offer a close-up view of how international businesspeople have managed the complexity and challenges they faced in U.S. markets. The case studies represent companies and entrepreneurs from countries including Australia, Colombia, Germany, Italy, the United Kingdom, South Korea, and more. Some were successful, others not so successful. Nonetheless, there are lessons to be learned that can be applied to your company and situation. In other words, my aim is for you to enter U.S. markets with eyes wide open.

In this introduction, I will outline my research and methodology, and I'll provide a chapter-by-chapter overview of what's to come in the book. Let's begin first by looking at the kinds of knowledge gaps I've typically seen among businesspeople when they first attempt to enter U.S. markets.

What International Entrants Need to Know

I first recognized a need for this book in 2016, when I was helping a French technology company, LumApps, enter the United States. It had sent a sales team, which had won dozens of European customers, to expand its U.S., Google-endorsed, software business. After 10 months, the team had secured only a few customers, and it was frustrated with the difficulty and expense of doing business here.

What the French company needed was help understanding U.S. market dynamics and business practices. Its problems weren't insurmountable. With some insight into the U.S. competitive environment and customers' purchase behavior, LumApps would be ready to craft and implement effective marketing and sales strategies. During a six-month consulting project, I worked with Rob Goldberg, a market research and new products expert, to interview dozens of potential customers and to map the competitive and market landscape. After we delivered our research and recommendations for marketing strategies, LumApps proceeded to penetrate the U.S. market with new customers and distribution partners. Its success was recognized by securing $70 million investment funds led by Goldman Sachs in 2020.[2]

In addition to consulting, I teach graduate courses in marketing and business strategy at Columbia University and New York University (NYU). Several years ago, I was asked to mentor members and give talks at two business-growth "accelerators," which nurture early-stage, pre-IPO companies and help international companies enter new U.S. markets. Both the Canadian Technology Accelerator and the WEVE Acceleration in New York City (which has more than 750 alumni from two decades helping international companies enter and scale in the United States) include in its membership startup and scale-up companies that had at least one immigrant founder or senior executive. These international executives and entrepreneurs struggled with marketing, sales, funding, legal issues, and managing U.S. employees.

My experience at these business accelerators further pointed to the need for a book on how to enter and scale businesses in U.S. markets—something that might offer a kind of "soft landing." As Frances Simowitz, chief executive officer (CEO) of WEVE Acceleration, said, "One of our jobs is to help foreign entrepreneurs to know what they don't know." The international students in my courses and the businesspeople I interviewed from around the globe confirmed a genuine interest in a practical book about what happens inside U.S. markets and enterprises.

Then in 2018, I worked as a strategy consultant on a rebranding project for the European American Chamber of Commerce in the United States (EACC-US), where several European chamber leaders encouraged me to write a book about doing business here. The organization, which we renamed as Leaders of European American Partnerships (LEAP), had been founded in 1990 to collaborate in providing education, resources, and local connections to European companies for bilateral business with U.S. organizations. The collective of 20 countries' chambers of commerce represents more than 25,000 companies, which account for the majority of business between the United States and Europe.

The European chamber leaders who helped inspire the writing of this book felt their organizations could be even more helpful, particularly in making connections, if foreign businesspeople were better prepared and informed. As Dietmar Rieg, CEO and president of the German American Chamber of Commerce, told me: International businesspeople need to "do their homework" because conducting business in the United States is so different than other countries.

More confirmation for the need for a book like this came my way. Federico Tozzi, executive director of the Italy-America Chamber of Commerce, told me one problem was that American news media focuses mainly on Washington, D.C., and New York, which makes it difficult for people overseas to learn about other areas in this vast country, particularly regarding U.S. consumers and market practices. And Fernanda Soza, executive director of Chile Massachusetts Alliance (ChileMass), said that foreign businesses desperately need more guides and cases studies. She noted that because the United States is so culturally different, people arriving from South America and other regions need guidance in areas such as cultural norms and explaining their products and solutions. Business in the United States, she said, is "very, very nuanced."

My Methodology

My first step was to investigate the areas that non-U.S. nationals wanted to learn about doing business in U.S. markets. In

December 2020, I sent a questionnaire to several hundred international business executives and entrepreneurs using WEVE's database and several LinkedIn groups. The questionnaire asked people about their aspirations and needs, including the following:

- Why is your company looking to expand to the U.S. market?
- What are the most important competencies to enter the U.S. market?
- What obstacles must a company overcome when trying to enter the U.S. market?
- What are the greatest knowledge gaps for companies entering the U.S. market?

Within a few weeks, I received about 65 responses to the questionnaire. The respondents were from companies that were distributed fairly equally between 1–10 employees, 11–49 employees, 50–250 employees, and more than 250 employees. While the sample size of this research was small, it did provide insights and direction to get me started. I discovered people most wanted to know about the following:

- Understanding U.S. consumers and clients
- Developing a marketing strategy for the United States
- Hiring and managing local talent
- Securing money to fund startups and U.S. expansions

What did they believe were their biggest obstacles to enter and scale in the U.S. market?

- Building trust and credibility with U.S. customers and partners
- Finding the funds to launch a product or service in the United States
- Navigating the complexity of U.S. regulatory, tax, and legal systems
- Obtaining visas to work and live in the United States

I then spent the next six months diving deeper into all of those topics. I found many answers in books, articles, and online publications. I learned even more by interviewing more than 100 people from 40 countries in 45-minute, recorded online sessions. People interviewed were from the following countries:

Africa	Egypt, Ethiopia, Nigeria, Tunisia
Asia and Middle East	China, India, Israel, Japan, Lebanon, Malaysia, Pakistan, South Korea, Sri Lanka, United Arab Emirates
Europe	Austria, Belgium, Czechia, Denmark, England, France, Ireland, Italy, Germany, Greece, Norway, Romania, Russia, Scotland, Spain, Sweden, Turkey, Ukraine
North America	Canada, Mexico, United States
Oceania	Australia
South America	Brazil, Costa Rica, Chile, Colombia

More than half of my interviewees were non-U.S. nationals at companies trying to enter or scale in U.S. markets. Their industries ranged from food and beverage, clothing, and financial services to medical devices, computer software, and transportation. They confirmed the knowledge gaps and perceived obstacles that my research questionnaire uncovered. For example, the founder of a digital media agency with three offices in Europe said the company wants "to go to the United States, but we don't know where to start!"

Other people interviewed were experienced accountants, lawyers, investors, and consultants in the United States who work with international companies. These professionals provided valuable information and recommendations on the process and potential pitfalls for U.S. expansion. Several experts worked mainly with startups, and they described the added challenges and requirements for early-stage companies led by foreign entrepreneurs.

How This Book Is Organized

I approached writing this book in a similar way to how I develop courses at universities. It starts with setting clear and measurable learning objectives, which guide the selection of topics, case studies, readings, and assignments. Reading this book, therefore, will allow you to do the following:

- Become familiar with U.S. business activities, requirements, and players
- Understand how American culture, business relationships, and marketing activities are unique and require different strategies and management skills
- Recognize the basics concepts of U.S. legal, tax, and immigration systems
- Identify and assess the capabilities needed to succeed in U.S. markets

With these learning objectives in mind, I selected which topics to cover and what tools and recommendations to present. After transcribing and analyzing the data from my interviews with 100+ people, I began writing, including facts and information uncovered from books, articles, and research reports. Each chapter also contains a short case study on an international company or entrepreneur followed with lessons to learn from the case. In addition, the appendixes contain three checklists to help prepare for your journey. And there is a glossary of terms used in American business.

The book unfolds as follows:

- Chapter 1 explains why the U.S. welcomes foreign companies and entrepreneurs—as well as some of the challenges involved in setting up shop here.
- Chapter 2 focuses on this question: Why try to enter and grow in the United States? This chapter examines eight reasons why the United States is the top choice for international business expansion and launching new businesses.

- Chapter 3 explores questions about the American Dream. What is it, where did it start, and is it attainable for foreign-born businesspeople and entrepreneurs?
- Chapter 4 tackles how to plan a successful U.S. expansion or business launch. It includes tools and frameworks to develop smart strategic plans.
- Chapter 5 answers this question: When is the best time to enter the U.S. market? It includes tools to help you determine market timing, and there's a U.S. Market Readiness Checklist in the Appendices.
- Chapter 6 addresses the question of what markets to prioritize and enter. It covers the nation's regional differences and factors to consider when selecting locations, product categories, and distribution channels.
- Chapter 7 focuses on legal questions, including business structures and intellectual property. It also explains why the U.S. legal system is unique and complicated.
- Chapter 8 covers how to finance your U.S. expansion or startup. It provides an overview of the different types of financing available as well as the financial institutions providing them.
- Chapter 9 explores U.S. culture and behaviors, in other words, how to understand Americans. It presents socio-cultural research and a framework to help you connect with people in this country.
- Chapter 10 examines the U.S. employment landscape and practices. It provides insights on how to build and manage teams as well as navigating the U.S. visa system.
- Chapter 11 addresses the question of how to establish a market presence here. It includes recommendations for branding and marketing to generate awareness and traction.

While I provide recommendations and best practices, you should consider these illustrative rather than rules. As Red Auerbach, coach of the Boston Celtics basketball teams that won nine NBA championships, said: "I never had a set of rules.

Every situation is different."[3] Your company and your personal situation are unique in many areas including resources, timing, and market dynamics.

Therefore, it is up to you to apply the learning from this book to your unique situation. And while you will need to assess and "grade" yourself, my sincere hope is that you will earn "high marks," demonstrated by undeniable success in U.S. markets.

Now let's launch into Chapter 1, where we begin with a proper American welcome—and a look at what to expect in terms of both the opportunities and challenges to be found here.

Source: Matthew Lee Sawyer photograph of American Clothing Company, Inc. box label

Notes

1. Obituary, *Newport Daily Express*, Newport Vermont, June 27, 1964.
2. "LumApps Raises $79 Million in Series C Funding led by Goldman Sachs," PR Newswire, January 22, 2020, https://www.prnewswire.com/news-releases/lumapps-raises-70-million-in-series-c-funding-led-by-goldman-sachs-300990842.html
3. Red Auerbach, Inspiring Quotes, Accessed December 4, 2021, https://www.inspiringquotes.us/quotes/vM3p_xWP4CZYI

1

Welcome to America

Welcome. We're glad you're thinking of bringing business here. You're in good company. The United States is the first place that international companies look to enter after they've established their business in their home country. It's no wonder; we're home to the largest and richest economy in the world where businesses of all types can grow to soaring heights, not only in profitable revenue but in stature and impact on the world.

If you're an entrepreneur, we're glad you want to start or scale your company here. The United States is the top choice for international startups. It's the first place non-U.S. companies want to scale after they've proven the business model in a smaller market. They know there is more investment money and a bigger startup community in the United States than anyplace in the world.

The United States is a great place for you personally to achieve your dreams, too. Anything is possible. You probably know about the Austrian bodybuilder with a funny name who became a successful movie star and Californian governor with a reported net worth of $400 million. You might not know that Arnold Schwarzenegger became a millionaire before movie stardom by starting a bricklaying business in California that he parlayed into a successful mail-order business selling Arnold Strong exercise equipment and instructional videos.[1]

Your success is important to us. The United States needs new blood—both new businesses and more people to fill jobs.

This chapter will describe some of what the United States has to offer in terms of opportunities, as well as some of the challenges involved in setting up shop here.

Let's begin with a look at what's needed when it comes to foreign startups and workers, and why.

Wanted: Fuel for Growth

Countries that do not have enough people to innovate and start up new businesses—and enough people to work in those businesses—can find their economies quickly falling behind. As captured in the 2019 news headline "Japan's Population Problem Is Straining Its Economy," that country's low birthrate and high longevity has led to an aging population and serious employment problems, which limit growth and the necessary income tax revenues to support its infrastructure.[2]

Today, the United States is beginning to face a similar "demographic stagnation." Apart from a general post-pandemic labor shortage, which may or may not prove temporary, the workforce of the future is already looking skimpy: the number of babies born in the United States is the lowest since 1979. Overall, the population of 331.4 million grew only 7.4 percent between 2010 and 2020, which is the smallest growth since the Great Depression in the 1930s. Notably, the number of Americans older than 55 grew 27 percent, compared to only 1.3 percent growth among people under 55.[3]

All of this points to an urgent need in the United States for foreigners to bring their businesses, ideas, and skilled labor into the country.

Businesses needed. The U.S. economy wouldn't be as strong without the contributions of immigrants and workers from other countries. Approximately 45 percent of the 500 largest U.S. companies were founded by immigrants or their children. They include Alphabet (parent company of Google), Biogen, DuPont, Kraft Heinz, and Pfizer. Together, these companies earned $4.2 trillion in revenue in 2018. That was $1.1 trillion more than Japan's total gross domestic product

(GDP), $2.1 trillion more than Germany's GDP, and nearly three times more than the United Kingdom's GDP.[4]

These companies founded by immigrants or their children provide good-paying jobs for U.S. workers. In 2019, these 222 companies employed 13.5 million people.[5] And international companies employed an additional 7.4 million U.S. workers.[6] But it isn't only those high employment numbers that matter. The *taxes* that workers in the United States pay enables our government to provide social programs, public education, infrastructure, military, and other programs to citizens.

In addition to new companies launching in the United States, we need established foreign businesses to open subsidiaries here. It helps the economy and creates new jobs for Americans. For example, MAS Holdings is a $2 billion revenue company based in Sri Lanka that designs, manufactures, and manages the supply chain for makers of textiles and clothing. Their customers include Calvin Klein, Lululemon, Victoria's Secret, and Nike. MAS Holdings established several U.S. companies starting in 2005 and today employs hundreds of U.S. workers—and more than 90 percent of them are tax-paying U.S. citizens.[7]

Entrepreneurs needed. The United States needs startup and scale-up companies to maintain our leadership in the industries of the future. Foreign-born entrepreneurs, engineers, and other talented individuals play an integral role. A study by the National Foundation for American Policy found that 50 of our $91 billion startups, referred to as *unicorns*, have at least one immigrant founder. SpaceX and Tesla were founded by South African–born Elon Musk. Other unicorn companies with immigrant founders include CrowdStrike, Uber, Zoom, and Warby Parker. Each of these companies employs a lot of people, too—an average of 1,200 workers.[8]

There are thousands of startups in industries ranging from business services and ecommerce to medical devices and solar energy. Entrepreneurs range in age, gender, ethnicity, location, education, and startup experience. They focus on rapid growth, and they're generally comfortable with ambiguity and higher risk. In *Startup Playbook*, industry veteran David Kidder notes that "while failure rates are very high, the ones that survive and thrive often produce outsized economic returns."[9]

Once the startup venture establishes its viability, either in the United States or another country, it looks to scale with increased revenue without a significant increase in people, capital, technology, and other resources. As explained by a successful venture capitalist, "growth is linear. Scaling-up is exponential growth." For example, a direct-to-consumer (DTC) business that focuses on using email solicitations to sell products can easily scale. They just need to send their electronic catalogs to a bigger list of people. The cost for creating the catalog and ecommerce site would be about the same, and the cost of goods should decrease on a per-unit basis. Those lower costs translate into higher profitability, too.

As Frances Simowitz of WEVE Acceleration colorfully put it: "Start-up babies have just an idea or an MVP (Minimum Viable Product). Scale-ups are like toddlers who want to run. They might be bumping into things, but they've got something there."

Workers needed. The United States needs foreign workers to keep our economy growing. Without workers for our manufacturing, healthcare, and other industries, our economy risks decline. Already we're facing significant shortages. According to a study by Deloitte and The Manufacturing Institute, more than 2 million manufacturing jobs will be unfilled through 2030. This worker shortage will limit our production, and it could cost the U.S. economy up to $1 trillion by 2030.[10]

Part of the problem is the demographic stagnation in the United States, already mentioned earlier in this chapter—the result of a decrease in the number of young people and an increase in older Americans. According to the U.S. Department for Health, the fertility rate—1.6 in 2020—has generally been below replacement for adult couples since 1971.[11] Farhad Manjoo wrote in *The New York Times* that such "demographic stagnation could bring its own high costs, among them a reduction in dynamism, productivity, and a slowdown in national and individual prosperity, even a diminishment of global power."[12]

One solution to this labor problem and demographic stagnation is immigrant workers. U.S. industry and infrastructure were built by the influx of working-age adults from other countries. Historically, several big immigration waves link directly to periods of U.S. economic growth. Notably, we can thank European, Asian, and more recently Hispanic immigrants for building much of our country's infrastructure and powerful industries.

During the coronavirus pandemic, immigrants and other foreigners played beneficial roles in two essential ways. First, we saw the importance of immigrant workers in the U.S. labor market. A large percentage of essential workers, who kept businesses functioning in everything from food service and construction to medical establishments, were first- and second-generation immigrants. Second, and crucially, foreign scientists in the United States, many visiting on H-1B visas, helped stop the pandemic. Eight companies developing the COVID-19 vaccine, including Johnson & Johnson and Regeneron, enlisted 3,310 foreign biochemists, biophysicists, chemists, and other scientists through the H-1B program. In addition, many of the doctors treating patients in hospitals throughout the pandemic were immigrants.[13]

Then, in 2021, the need for workers grew when many Americans decided to retire early or leave the workforce. According to U.S. Labor Department data, there were 10 million job openings, and most industries had more job openings than qualified workers to fill them.[14] Business owners of all sizes raised pay to entice people to reenter the workforce or switch careers.

Expect Some Hurdles

Despite the great need for foreign businesses in the United States, actually doing business here can be difficult. Many international companies try to enter U.S. markets only to give up after a few years, having lost money, time, and reputation. Most startups fail after a few years, too. Forbes reported that historically 90 percent of startups fail within 10 years.[15]

Why are there so many failures? International businesspeople and entrepreneurs told me that they underestimated the difficulty, cost, and length of time required to enter the U.S. market. They complain about the confusing tax and business regulations that can vary widely among our 50 states. Competition with established and new companies can be fierce.

> "There are a lot of challenges and complexities about doing business in the United States," said Matthias Farwick, CEO of Txture, an Austrian technology company that is trying to enter the U.S. market with a cloud transformation platform. "It's difficult to grasp the gravity of these challenges until you've actually experienced them. After I lived it, now I know."[16]

Here is a list of just some of the hurdles a new foreign entrant might face in the United States:

- **Problems getting established.** Gemma Cortijo, executive director of the Spain-U.S. Chamber of Commerce, described how international executives often face difficulties with basic needs. For example, because they don't have a credit history in the United States, they have trouble opening a bank account and getting a credit card. Dealing with financial institutions is one of the areas where chambers of commerce are able to provide guidance and support, particularly when an individual doesn't have a history accessing U.S. credit.[17]
- **Difficulties pitching ideas.** American consumers and business clients can be demanding and impatient. Business-to-business (B2B) salespeople complain that it's hard to get a foot in the door to sell their products and services. And if they do get an appointment, they get only a few minutes to deliver their pitch. Startups usually get even less time. That's why it is a good idea to create a one- or two-minute pitch of your business idea that you can practice and be ready to deliver to a decision-maker informally, if

necessary. (It's called an *elevator pitch*—so named because it's short and succinct enough to be delivered while traveling between a lobby and the prospect's office.)

- **Need for resources.** Capital and resources are often in short supply at startups and scale-ups. (I once worked for a budget-constrained technology startup where we had to bring our own tea bags to the office.) The entrepreneurial world requires a higher degree of perseverance and dedication. Bruce Buchanan, CEO of Australian startup Rokt, said, "The early days are tough. It's hard to get traction and credibility. You don't have a network; you don't have access to people that can help you when you're starting from scratch. So, you got to have a lot of grit and stubbornness and resilience." (Learn more about Rokt in the case study in Chapter 2.)
- **The challenge of living—and staying—in the United States.** It's not an easy personal decision to move to the United States. Housing and living costs are more expensive than most countries. There are many challenges to setting up a life here, particularly for immigrants. Even if you went to an American university and are already living here, you may have difficulty securing a new visa to stay longer.

It's Worth It!

Despite the challenges, bringing your strong business concept and talents to the United States is worth the effort. (For a detailed example of the ups and downs experienced by one entrepreneur, see the case study on MediaCom at the end of this chapter.)

In the next chapter, I'll present eight reasons why the United States is the best place to scale your business. If you're an entrepreneur, the most compelling reason will be the oversized potential return on investment. But first the promised case study.

Case Study: MediaCom (Colombia)

Juan Pablo Gnecco ran a digital photography business in Colombia. Despite having steady work, he found it difficult to pay his eight employees and support a family. Juan Pablo decided to apply to marketing jobs in the United States, and he received an offer from one in Atlanta, Georgia. So in 1995, Juan Pablo, his wife, and three young children packed up their suitcases and moved to the United States. Their clothes fit into eight suitcases and toys filled two more.

Upon arrival in Atlanta, Juan Pablo found the marketing agency was having financial difficulties, and the job never materialized. Although this was discouraging, he also knew that the Olympics were coming to Atlanta the next year. He was certain there would be plenty of work for someone with strong digital photography and multimedia skills.

Determined to make it in America, Juan Pablo met with anyone who might need a photographer or art director. He picked up freelance projects and started to hang out at Georgia Tech's Media Lab. This was during the first days of the Internet, and GT's Media Lab was an early pioneer. Juan Pablo's keen sense of design and photography helped them build beautiful websites for Georgia Power and other companies in Atlanta.

The innovative work produced at Media Lab caught the attention of a fast-growing interactive marketing agency called iXL. The agency had 30 employees at the time, in 1996, and within three years iXL had 1,500 employees and more than $100 million revenue. Juan Pablo accepted a job offer from iXL, which he saw as an opportunity to learn the "ins and outs" of doing business in the United States. As he said, "I had run a business for years in Colombia, but I had no experience in how it was done in the United States."[18]

In January 1998, Juan Pablo left iXL to start his own agency, MediaCom. To keep costs low, his team of three worked out of his family's apartment. The agency was one of the first to incorporate animated graphics and online games to make websites more fun and visually interesting. This led to projects for Turner Broadcasting's Cartoon Network. To keep costs low and speed delivery, Juan Pablo hired freelance programmers and digital engineers. He found their "magic recipe" was to support U.S. clients from Atlanta and accelerate the production by employing freelance technologists in Bogota, Colombia.

In 1999 MediaCom was asked to build a holiday website for Coca-Cola's Christmas message. Juan Pablo and his team impressed their client with a great design and quick turnaround on some major changes that the company requested. The footage for the original website had been filmed outdoors, but two weeks before launch the Coca-Cola executives thought Santa should be dancing and playing indoors. This meant totally reshooting the footage. Juan Pablo's response? "No problem, we can get it done in time."

Soon after, Juan Pablo was asked to bid on another Coca-Cola project that was worth $2.4 million. At the time, MediaCom's revenue was $1 million. For the pitch meeting, Juan Pablo included two ex-Coca-Cola executives who knew how the big company worked. The company won the project, and the two executives came on board to manage the relationship. Soon MediaCom won additional multimillion-dollar projects for two more brands in the Coca-Cola family.

Two years later, MediaCom opened a Boston office to support a $6 million assignment from Dunkin Donuts. Then, after winning a project for Mattel's Barbie, MediaCom expanded in Los Angeles with an office of 10 people.

(*continued*)

(*continued*)

However, expanding the business and satisfying the demands of clients was costly. Juan Pablo tried to cut back on administrative staff, but it wasn't enough to keep up with the growing payroll needed to produce the work. The company soon was facing severe cash flow problems and needed to secure investment money.

In 2005 MediaCom was bought by the world's largest advertising company WPP for more than $10 million. WPP merged Juan Pablo's agency with VML, a digital agency based in Kansas City, to help them attract bigger clients. The agency soon added other premier clients including the American Cancer Society, Sony Digital, SABMiller, Philips Electronics, and Twentieth Century Fox. By 2010, MediaCom had grown from about 50 people to more than 200.

Juan Pablo didn't forget his Colombian roots. In 2001, he and his wife helped create and provide funding for the Colombianitos Foundation in Bogota. Over the past 20 years, the nonprofit organization has helped more than 135,000 children in more than 100 locations through sports programs promoting citizenship, leadership, gender equality, and prevention of alcohol abuse.[19]

Juan Pablo downplays the difficulty of being an immigrant entrepreneur in America. He thinks people shouldn't be so worried about jumping into the U.S. market. "You have to learn a lot of things, and you are going to bump your head against the walls. But you will find that it's a lot less difficult than doing anything in Columbia. For every single company in Colombia, you can do 10 companies here."

As Juan Pablo said, "There's such an opportunity here. This country is so extremely generous and open to allow foreign businesses to flourish here. I mean, it's really the American Dream."

Lessons from This Case Study

1. **Adopt an American-style of networking.** Upon arriving in Atlanta, Juan Pablo went to art and networking events where he introduced himself to everyone. He showed them his photography portfolio and talked about building websites. They were impressed with his friendly, energetic, and positive personality—quintessentially "American"!
2. **Find advocates and business partners.** Juan Pablo's connections led to meeting people on the cutting edge of Internet technology at Georgia Tech. This network led to his being hired at iXL and meeting potential clients for his own agency.
3. **Have a plan and follow it.** Juan Pablo had a plan, a clear goal, and the drive to succeed. He developed expertise in digital photography and multimedia communication. He learned how businesses ran in the United States by working for others. He built and sold a multimillion-dollar business by winning one client at a time.
4. **Don't underestimate the importance of timing.** Juan Pablo went to Atlanta just as the city was needing digital photography for the Olympics. He was fortunate to catch the Internet wave when there was an insatiable need for technology-savvy, creative people and agencies.

Notes

1. Tom Reimann, "30 Surprising Facts About Arnold Schwarzenegger," Collider, May 10, 2019, collider.com/galleries/30-surprising-facts-about-arnold-schwarzenegger
2. Yuko Takeo and Hannah Dormido, "Japan's Population Problem Is Straining Its Economy," Bloomberg, September 19, 2019, www.bloomberg.com/graphics/2019-japan-economy-aging-population
3. William Frey, "What the 2020 Census Will Reveal About America," Brookings, January 11, 2021, www.brookings.edu/research/what-the-2020-census-will-reveal-about-america-stagnating-growth-an-aging-population-and-youthful-diversity

4. Benjamin Fearnow, "Nearly Half of All Fortune 500 Companies Were Founded By Immigrants or Their Children, Study Finds," *Newsweek*, July 22, 2019, www.newsweek.com/immigrant-founded-fortune-500-companies-us-gdp-1450498
5. Ibid.
6. National FDI Data, "Foreign Direct Investment Strengthens America's Economy," Global Business Alliance, December 2, 2021, globalbusiness.org/factsheet/national-fdi-data
7. Conversation with Surein Wijeyeratne, chief communication officer, MAS Holdings, on April 21, 2021
8. Stuart Anderson, "55% Of America's Billion-Dollar Startups Have An Immigrant Founder," *Forbes*, February 3, 2019, www.forbes.com/sites/stuartanderson/2018/10/25/55-of-americas-billion-dollar-startups-have-immigrant-founder
9. David Kidder, *The Startup Playbook* (San Francisco: Chronicle Books, 2012), p. 13.
10. Matt Egan, "American Factories Are Desperate For Workers. It's a $1 Trillion Problem," CNN Business, May 4. 2021, www.cnn.com/2021/05/04/economy/manufacturing-jobs-economy/index.html
11. Bill Chappell, "U.S. Birthrate Fell By 4% in 2020: Hitting Another Record Low," NPR.org, May 04, 2021, www.npr.org/2021/05/05/993817146/u-s-birth-rate-fell-by-4-in-2020-hitting-another-record-low
12. Farhad Manjoo, "The World Might Be Running Low on Americans," *New York Times*, May 20, 2021, www.nytimes.com/2021/05/20/opinion/the-world-might-be-running-low-on-americans.html
13. Fact Sheet, "The H-1B Visa Program," American Immigration Council, May 26, 2021, www.americanimmigrationcouncil.org/research/h1b-visa-program-fact-sheet
14. Heather Long, et al., "Why America has 8.4 Million Unemployed When There Are 10 Million Job Openings, *Washington Post*, Sep. 4, 2021, www.washingtonpost.com/business/2021/09/04/ten-million-job-openings-labor-shortage/
15. Neil Patel, "90% of Startups Fail: Here's What You Need to Know About the 10%," *Forbes*, January 6, 2015, www.forbes.com/sites/neilpatel/2015/01/16/90-of-startups-will-fail-heres-what-you-need-to-know-about-the-10/?sh=187d3b946679
16. Conversation with Mathias Fenwick, founder and CEO of Txture, on April 7, 2021
17. Conversation with Gemma Cortijo, executive director of Spain-U.S. Chamber of Commerce, on February 10, 2021
18. Conversation with Juan Pablo Gnecco, founder of MediaCom, on April 1, 2021
19. "Leaders in the Use of Sports as a Tool for Social Transformation," Fundación Colombianitos, Accessed May 20, 2021, colombianitos.org/en/curriculos-2

2

Why the United States?

Recently, the president of an Eastern European company that manufactures home appliances asked my advice on whether to branch into the United States or another country. He'd heard stories that doing business in the United States is difficult, competitors are fierce, and it's expensive. Other international businesspeople have asked me similar questions. All wondered whether the United States was in decline. The "land of opportunity," it seems, has not been living up to its reputation for offering prosperity and personal happiness.

Yes, there's no doubt the image of the United States has diminished over the past decade or so. Some might say our gold-standard brand has tarnished. Certainly, we've had plenty of problems: divided political tribes, intensified racial unrest, deeper income disparity, too many guns. Heck, even Superman has shied away from being a U.S.-only superhero. In 2021, DC Comics announced that it was changing the Man of Steel's motto from "Truth, Justice, and the American Way" to "Truth, Justice, and a Better Tomorrow."

Nonetheless, the United States still promises more opportunities for business growth and personal fulfillment than anywhere else in the world. This chapter presents the argument for why the United States is the most desirable country for international startups and scale-ups. It includes a case study about an Australian startup company and its lessons learned while establishing a U.S. presence. Later chapters will explore where, when, and how to enter and scale your business. But first, let's examine eight key reasons why you should consider exerting the time, resources, and effort on the U.S. market.

Reason #1: Biggest Market in the World

The most obvious reason to do business in the United States is the size and consistent growth of its economic market. Market size determines the total revenue potential as it sets a ceiling or upper limit to expansion. The bigger the market, the bigger the opportunity. In the words of one global investment banker, the U.S. market offers "almost infinite upside."

Indeed, the U.S. economy is the biggest in the world, with $24 trillion gross domestic product (GDP) in 2021.[1] That was approximately $10 trillion, or 70 percent bigger than the second largest economy, China. (Note that the U.S. GDP dipped to $20.9 trillion in 2020 due to the COVID pandemic, but it quickly bounced back.) In other words, if you don't do business in the United States, you're missing out on the customers and resources that represent a full one-third of the entire world's economy.

Regional and state economic markets in the United States are huge, too. The state of California alone, with a GDP of $2.7 trillion, ranks as the world's fifth-largest economy—bigger than that of the whole United Kingdom. Texas, at $1.7 trillion GDP, is the size of world's 10th-largest economy. That's bigger than the economy of Canada.[2] Several U.S. cities have enormous economies, too: New York City's comes in at $1.7 trillion GDP; Los Angeles has a $1.1 trillion GDP; and Chicago's GDP is $.7 trillion.[3]

Market size is especially important in the startup and scale-up worlds. Venture capital (VC) executives maintain that the total potential demand, or market size, determines how big an early-stage company can grow and scale with the least amount of friction.[4] In fact, VCs' first consideration when evaluating a company's potential is the size of the market it is entering.

Specifically, investors want to know the total addressable market (TAM), which represents the total potential sales if your product or service has 100 percent market share. The TAM is fairly easy to calculate once you have the data. Let's say your company sells toothbrushes. The TAM for toothbrushes is the number of people with teeth to brush. The United States is the third most-populous country, after China and India, with 331 million people.[5] American dentists generally recommend replacing toothbrushes every three to four months. Therefore, the TAM for toothbrushes in the United States is more than a billion per year.

Market size is considered more important than the management team, and it is more important than the product or service. Some VC firms won't invest in a venture unless it has the potential to return 10 times (or 1,000 percent) of their investment. That's because, as VC investors say, it is easy to fix the product and somewhat easy to change the management team, but you can't change the market.

Reason #2: Strong and Stable

The strength and stability of the U.S. economy and dollar make it exceptionally conducive for doing business. The U.S. economic expansion, starting in 2010 and running for more than a decade, was the longest on record. Moreover, the future looks bright: *The Economist* has predicted continued economic expansion well into the current decade, due to rock-steady growth in consumer spending coupled with higher wages for workers.[6]

Ruchir Sharma, chief global strategist at Morgan Stanley Investment Management, predicted the United States will continue to be the world's top financial superpower. In a 2020 article titled "The Comeback Nation; U.S. Economic Supremacy has Repeatedly Proved Declinists Wrong," Sharma reports the U.S. share of the global economy has held steady at 25 percent for four decades. During the same period, the European Union declined from 35 percent to 21 percent, and Japan dropped from 10 percent to 6 percent. Although China grew from 2 percent to 16 percent, its growth did not come at U.S. expense.[7]

The strong U.S. dollar is both a result of and contributor to economic market strength. Almost 90 percent of global financial transactions through banks are conducted using the U.S. dollar—even when no U.S. parties are involved. Because the U.S. Federal Reserve Bank controls the supply of dollars, it is the world's central bank. This "reserve currency status" ensures there is a steady demand for dollars, and it enables the United States to borrow cheaply, through government bonds, from other countries.[8]

Such strength and resilience in the U.S. economy have held steady—despite its massive size—even after economic downturns. One reason for this strength is swift government actions to get the economy growing again. After the 1929 stock market crash and the ensuing economic depression, President Franklin D. Roosevelt instituted banking system reforms and New Deal programs that got people back to work. After the 2008–2009 financial credit crisis, President Barack Obama resuscitated the economy with the Troubled Asset Relief Program (TARP) and other programs to boost businesses. What's more, swift and substantial government action led to a quick U.S. economic recovery from the 2020 pandemic. Allen Sinai, chief global economist and strategist at Decision Economics, Inc., called the phenomenon "a collapse and then a boom-like pickup."[9]

Startup ecosystems in the United States have proven to be resilient and strong. Two years after the 2008–2009 recession, employment in the computer systems industry grew at a 3 percent annual rate from its pre-crisis level, while the overall job market growth was negative, at -1.2%, according to Startup Genome data.[10] And even during this recession, several unicorns were launched, including Airbnb, Beyond Meat, Instagram, Uber, and Warby Parker.

Reason #3: Access to Customers

Access to a large pool of potential customers is important for companies that need to grow very quickly. If you are selling a food, fashion, entertainment, or any consumer product, then you'll want to sell to U.S. customers. Americans love to shop and spend money. U.S. families purchased more than $13.3 trillion in goods and services in 2017. While comprising only 4 percent of the world's population, U.S. consumers account for more than one-quarter of the entire world's household consumption.[11]

Indeed, most U.S. citizens have money to spend. Disposable income, calculated as gross income minus Social Security contributions and income taxes, was an average of $55,613 for U.S. citizens older than 15 years of age in May 2021.[12] Since the United States is not one homogenous economic market, we need to be careful when looking at averages and aggregate numbers. One glaring example is the country's unequal distribution of wealth. According to the United States Federal Reserve, people in the top 1 percent economic bracket hold 31 percent of the wealth in the country, which accounted for $36.6 trillion in December 2020. The bottom 50 percent of Americans hold only 2 percent, roughly $2.5 trillion, of our country's wealth.[13]

Among the products that Americans love to buy are new foods and beverages, especially those from other countries and cultures. The average U.S. supermarket has 28,112 items on its shelves. Mintel Group tracked that companies introduced more than 20,000 new food and beverage products in the United States during each year between 2016 and 2020.[14] Americans also love new films, music, and art from around the globe. Foreign-created entertainment satisfies American's desire to show friends and social media networks their sophistication and worldly knowledge.

If you are selling business products or services, then you'll want to sell to the world's largest business-to-business (B2B) market. There are approximately 30 million U.S. businesses with more than one employee, and more than 20,000 with more than 50 employees.[15] A study of European and Israeli business founders by Index Ventures revealed that 78 percent of people ranked "access to customers" as the top reason for expansion into the United States.[16] The large customer base is the primary reason the Australian company Rokt entered the United States shortly after its launch. (See Rokt's story in the case study at the end of this chapter.)

U.S. businesses are also eager to experiment and try new technologies. Large companies have budgets and teams to regularly test new technology-based solutions. Forrester Research predicts that U.S. business and government agencies will spend $1.9 trillion on technology goods and services in 2021, with $431 billion on computer software alone. They also predict that new technology projects will grow 8 percent in 2021 and 12 percent in 2022.[17]

Consider, for example, the U.K.-based company 3 Sided Cube, which creates apps and digital products for corporate social responsibility (CSR) efforts, such as responding to natural disasters and combating deforestation. When revenues from U.S. clients (including the American Red Cross, Accenture, and Nordstrom) reached a critical mass—comprising a full half of its total revenues—the company decided to open an office in Chicago. As Sophia "Puff" Story, a 3 Sided Cube co-founder, explained, the company needed to be physically closer to its customers and respond faster to incoming sales leads, which were mostly from U.S. organizations.[18]

Reid Hoffman, serial entrepreneur and VC executive, coined the term *blitzscaling* to describe this focus on scaling a company and its customer base. Why? From a strategically "offensive" viewpoint, rapid growth can lead to market leadership and higher valuations. His company, LinkedIn, wasn't valuable until it reached scale with millions of users. Likewise, low-margin businesses, such as Amazon and PayPal, weren't profitable until they gained millions of customers. From a defensive strategic viewpoint, companies want to reach and acquire customers before their competitors do, so they can enjoy lower costs and other advantages of scale.[19]

Reason #4: Pro-Business Environment

The United States has been, and always will be, conducive to business and commerce. The country was founded for business reasons, as the 13 colonies banded together for economic strength. You've probably heard of the Boston Tea Party in

1773, when American patriots dumped 342 chests of imported tea to protest unfair taxes imposed by the British East India Company. In other colonies, business-minded farmers, including future President George Washington, rebelled against British control of the tobacco markets.

Throughout the nation's almost 250-year history, one of government's primary roles has been to facilitate the growth and prosperity of our free market economy. Presidents win and lose elections based on how well they've enabled businesses to grow. Ronald Reagan captured the presidency in 1980 from incumbent Jimmy Carter when he asked voters, "Are you better off today than you were four years ago?" The Republican Party promotes itself as the party of small government and big business. Yet the Democratic Party is also pro-business and growth-minded; in fact, democratic President Joe Biden won in counties that represented more than 70 percent of the country's economic output.[20]

While there might be talk about protecting U.S. manufacturing jobs from foreign competition, in reality the country has made it relatively easy for international companies to build U.S. factories. Two of the top three automobiles with the most U.S.-made components and assembly in 2018 were from the Japanese Honda Motor company.[21] Foreign companies have a U.S. presence in virtually every category, from financial services and food to pharmaceuticals. In fact, 7.9 million U.S. citizens are employed by international companies.[22]

Moreover, in the World Bank's annual "Doing Business" report, the United States ranked fifth, tied with South Korea with 84.0, out of 190 countries for "ease of doing business." The top country, New Zealand, scored only slightly higher, at 86.8.[23] The study analyzes government regulations and processes that promote efficiency and support freedom to do business in five areas.

- Setting up a business
- Getting a location, including securing building permits and electricity
- Accessing financing

- Dealing with day-to-day operations
- Operating in a secure environment

The United States also favors entrepreneurs. In the "Best Countries to Start a Business" list, it ranks fourth in the world.[24] The three countries ahead of the United States are Singapore, Indonesia, and Mexico. This yearly ranking by *U.S. News and World Report* is based on a global survey from 4,919 business decision-makers on five attributes.

- Affordability
- Level of bureaucracy
- Manufacturing costs
- Connections to the rest of the world
- Easy access to capital

Reason #5: Access to Money

Since money is critical to fund business activities, other U.S. strengths are the amount of available capital, the diversity of money sources, and the risk appetite of the investment organizations. With the largest economy and largest financial institutions, there is an ample pool of liquid capital to tap. In addition, many U.S. government organizations offer tax incentives and access to capital. Chapter 8 covers funding options and strategies, but here are some highlights on why the United States is the top place for accessing money.

Companies can raise money by issuing stock traded in public equity markets or private equity firms. The United States has the biggest and strongest capital markets by far. The New York Stock Exchange (NYSE) and the NASDAQ account for 46 percent of the $89.5 trillion global stock market value. In the decade between 2010 and 2020, U.S. stock markets rose by 250 percent, which was nearly four times the gain in other national stock markets.[25]

The U.S. stock and bond markets are open to companies and investors from virtually every country. There are more than 500 non-U.S. companies on the NYSE—including Alibaba, Toyota, and Sony—representing 46 countries. Didi Global, the Chinese ride-sharing company, chose to issue its IPO on the NYSE in July 2021. International companies know that U.S. stock markets offer prestige and a sense of legitimacy in addition to capital.

Entrepreneurs and early-stage companies raise money before going public through venture capital and private investors and investment funds. Even in the midst of the pandemic in 2020, U.S. companies backed by venture capital (VC) raised half ($129.7 billion) of the total global venture funding ($259 billion).[26] Entrepreneurs find funding through a wide range of sources in the United States, including angel investors, incubators, accelerators, strategic investors at corporations, and debt investors.

U.S. investors are known for their willingness to take risks. Because the U.S. market is so huge, there is the opportunity for huge financial returns. Some VC firms won't back a venture unless they can realize 10 times (1,000 percent) return on their investment. Other investors evaluate the "opportunity cost," which is the potential lost profit if the firm *doesn't* invest in a particular project.

In addition, many states, regions, cities, and municipalities offer international companies tax incentives to place their business in their location. They know that new businesses help the local economy and employ local citizens. Some locales have an Economic Development Organization (EDO) to help manage government processes and secure funds with local banks and private investors. Increasingly, EDOs have focused on helping startups and entrepreneurs. They have created many programs, such as New York State's Start-up NY, to help entrepreneurs and early-stage companies with funding, education, office space, and other resources.

Reason #6: Access to Talent

Capable and talented people are the heart, soul, and lifeblood for every company. All the leading digital technology companies are in competition to attract the best talent. Some claim that a computer programmer who ranks among the top 10 percent can produce *10 times* more code than an average programmer. Management, sales, and legal skills are also in high demand. The United States is home to millions of the brightest and highest skilled workers. They include U.S.-born and immigrants who arrived to study or to work.

U.S. universities have long been considered the best in the world. The country is home to eight of the top 10–rated schools in the world.[27] These schools all have huge endowments—Harvard's is $36 billion, and the University of Texas has $26.5 billion—so they can afford the best facilities, research equipment, and highest-paid faculty. These schools also can afford generous scholarships to attract the best students from around the world. It's no wonder that technology, medical, and other advanced industries started and are located nearby leading institutions. Silicon Valley has Stanford University. Boston has M.I.T. and Harvard. New York City has Columbia and New York University.

Communities of talented people share ideas, resources, and best practices. Healthy competition among peers also leads to stronger companies and innovative new products. Justin Kan, founder of Twitch, which was bought by Amazon for $970 million, talked about the value of the U.S. entrepreneurial ecosystem. It's a "massive secondary ecosystem of people who have scaled before. They've scaled the technical side. They've scaled the operations side. That knowledge isn't as readily available in the rest of the world. Coming here and talking to experts who have done it before, learning from them, and getting them on your side through an investment is a great way to accelerate your progress."[28]

Reason #7: Openness to New People and Ideas

Despite some political rhetoric about "America First" and reports of cultural discord, the United States has, and always will be, open to immigrants. Americans recognize the country was founded and built by immigrants over the past 300 years. Each year, millions of people immigrate to the United States for purposes including studying, working, and escaping persecution in their home country. Some are here temporarily, while others seek permanent citizenship.

Moreover, the majority of U.S. citizens support the idea of immigration. A 2018 Pew Research study found that 68 percent of U.S. citizens believe "openness to people from all over the world is essential to who we are as a nation." This was especially true among young adults (aged 18–29 years old): 80 percent agreed with that statement. Among people with college or post-graduate degree educations, 76 percent agreed. Only 26 percent of the people surveyed believed that "if America is too open to people from around the world, then we risk our identity as a nation."[29]

Sparks & Honey (S&H), a consulting firm that specializes in cultural trends, reports the United States is increasingly open and welcoming to outside people and ideas. "Things that once seemed alternative, eccentric or fringe are now being translated into new standards in policy, communication and creative expression."[30] S&H viewed this trend as a result of political extremes and natural disasters that have made people feel unstable and insecure. "With the world in uncertain flux, we feel freer to embrace boundary-free identities and to adopt new means to accommodate the divergent perspectives of an ever-wider range of people."

Non-U.S. nationals who want to join the U.S. workforce generally find a welcoming environment here. Over the last decades, businesses have come to recognize that diversity of their workforce and practices leads to higher profitability. McKinsey studied more than 1,000 large companies on their diversity and inclusion practices, and they found the top quartile outperformed the bottom quartile by 36 percent in profitability.[31]

While starting a business is never easy, immigrants experience Americans to be helpful and open. Entrepreneur Christian

Chemaly found people in New York to be extremely open minded and willing to help his technology startup. Christian was born in Lebanon and moved to the United States after living in Europe. About NYC, he said, "It's a city that accepts foreigners much easier than others. I lived in London, Hamburg, Berlin, and Paris. I never felt the integration as much as here."[32]

"I have been welcomed with open arms," said Scott Weir, CEO of property management company Pillow Partners founded in Glasgow, Scotland, which has expanded into the United States. "I think if you're positive and bring value to the business community, you get a very warm welcome from Americans."[33]

Reason #8: Proven Global Leadership

Because the level of competition and market demands in the United States require strong organizations and leaders, people view business success in America as proof they can be successful anywhere. Product success in the United States is considered proof it is viable in most other markets.

Proof of product viability and market penetration is particularly important for technology and science-driven products. Only products of the highest quality and value are able to succeed in the United States, said Sree Sivanandan, a venture growth partner and investor based in India. He explained that doing business in the United States provides a level of safety for risk-averse purchasers of sophisticated technology.[34] Sree used the analogy of getting approval for a medicine to be administered across the world: If the U.S. Federal Drug Administration (FDA) approves the medicine, that "OK" provides every medical practitioner in the world with the confidence they need to prescribe it safely. Similarly, if a software company based in South Asia has clients in the United States, it will lead to sales in other countries. Sree said this is especially true when companies want to sell a product based on quality rather than low price.

Success in the United States proves the long-term viability and growth for global organizations. Research found "if firms are successful with [U.S.] entry, it is likely they will grow faster and survive longer." The group of scholars concluded that the earlier a firm goes international, the more capable they are for growing in multiple foreign markets. Managing competitive and changing market conditions develops their ability to adapt to uncertain environments. Since the United States is highly competitive and constantly changing, entering the U.S. market "exposes a firm to opportunities to grow and to learn how to grow."[35]

More Reasons to Come

These eight are the rational and logical reasons why to bring your business and your talents to the United States. Since most decisions include individuals' emotional and personal reasons as well, the next chapter focuses on one from the heart: the American Dream.

But first, here is the case study of an Australian company that chose to enter the United States for smart and logical reasons. Not to spoil the story, but things turned out well for this unicorn company.

Case Study: Rokt (Australia)

Rokt is a software development company founded by Australian entrepreneur Bruce Buchanan. The company's mission is to make ecommerce smarter, faster, and better. The ecommerce software market, estimated at $6 billion in 2020, is projected to grow to $20 billion by 2028.[36] That rapid growth is due to companies increasingly selling their consumer and B2B products through online websites and mobile applications. Even companies dedicated

(*continued*)

(continued)

to physical retail stores jumped into selling through online websites during the COVID-19 pandemic.

Bruce discovered the importance of ecommerce software early in the game. Prior to Rokt, he was CEO of Jetstar Airways, the largest low-fare airline throughout Asia. Jetstar was one of the first direct-to-consumer (DTC) companies utilizing the World Wide Web. The formula proved profitable indeed: In 2012, at the time of Bruce's departure after 10 years at Jetstar, the airline employed about 14,000 people across 17 countries, with revenues around $4 billion.

How did Jetstar do it? Bruce and his team realized if they could optimize the transaction experience when people are buying tickets online, they could transform the profitability of the airline industry. When they couldn't find adequate software technology, they started to develop their own. The technology was complicated; ecommerce transactions require many third parties to interact at the transaction moment. The technology required extensive research and development (R&D) with a large team of digital technologists and software engineers, including experts in advanced machine learning (ML) and artificial intelligence (AI). Since the requirements kept growing and changing, Jetstar's software development costs didn't end after the initial system was built.

Bruce recognized this problem wasn't limited to the airline industry. Virtually every company selling online could increase profits if they improved and personalized the customer checkout experience. Research shows that 70 percent of consumers abandon online shopping carts before completing their purchase.[37] And even if customers complete the purchase, most ecommerce sites don't capitalize on potential sales from complementary products.

Bruce felt there was a great opportunity for a new company that could "crack this problem."

In 2012, Bruce bought a small business in Australia that was serving one ecommerce client. While he ultimately intended to create a global company, he knew he had to build it one country at a time. His new business, Rokt, started in Australia by building and testing its solutions for several clients. After achieving successful results, Rokt expanded into New Zealand and then Singapore after the first year.

Several clients in Australia, including Ticketmaster, wanted Rokt to help their U.S. business operations. To expand overseas, Rokt secured $8 million in Series A funding in 2013 from Square Peg Capital, based in Australia. The investors believed in Rokt's product as well as Bruce's leadership and business acumen. They based their investment bet, though, primarily on the opportunity to dramatically scale Rokt's business with the large pool of U.S. ecommerce companies.

As Bruce explained, "From day one, I knew we had to come to the United States. I worked really hard to build the base business product with the R&D team in Sydney. And once we accomplished that in the first 12 months, we got funding to start the U.S. growth."[38]

For the next two years, Bruce traveled regularly to the United States to develop business with top ecommerce decision-makers. He said it was hard to get traction and credibility in the beginning because Rokt didn't have a wide network of connections to potential customers. Therefore, they leveraged their strength in the travel and ticketing industries to build a base of clients. While he was commuting, Rokt hired several sales and customer support people, which led to opening a New York office in 2014. Then, in 2015, Bruce transitioned the company head

(*continued*)

(*continued*)

office from Sydney to New York City and moved to the United States with his family.

When asked why he relocated to the United States, Bruce said, "That's easy. It's the market. If you want to be the global leader in any category, you have to be in the States." He also expressed, "I think you have to be all in; you have to really commit. You must be nimble and responsive to market feedback, and you have to have an unnerving belief that you're going to solve customers' most difficult problems. That's a hard challenge to solve without a deep commitment."

Although Rokt later opened offices in San Francisco and Los Angeles, they closed within two years because the executive team found it was easier to manage and coordinate with the entire U.S. team working together in New York City. Since each customer sale was sizable, they could afford to put salespeople on planes when needed. Also, many of the largest ecommerce customers were located in the New York area.

In the beginning, Rokt executives found that managing activities between the United States and Australia was especially challenging because of the 14-hour difference in time zones. When Rokt eventually moved time-sensitive functions from Sydney to New York City, Bruce said the move was a "critical piece of the puzzle" to its success.

Bruce was careful about who he brought into the organization, looking for people who could solve problems with resilience, toughness, and grit. He wanted people on his team who could conquer new frontiers—people he called "curious explorers." People who were willing to fight for something that can be tough. "Because when you're building something from the ground up, or you're trying to migrate a business from another country to the United States, a lot of things are going to be bloody tough."

One of Rokt's first hires in the United States, in 2015,was Ashley Robinson from New Jersey. Only two years out of college, Ashley was hired as an account manager. It wasn't an easy job, as clients expected issues to be resolved quickly and efficiently. The R&D team in Australia weren't accustomed to the pace of U.S. business. But for Ashley, no problem was too tough, and no client was too demanding. She was eager to accept new roles and responsibilities. Ashley was promoted to vice president in 2017, and she was promoted to senior vice president of customer success in 2020.

In 2020, Rokt claimed more than $100 million in revenue with plans to grow from 260 to 400 employees by the end of 2021.[39] Then the company secured $325 million funds in 2021 and was valued at $1.95 billion.[40] With a corporate head office in New York City, Rokt does business in the United States, Australia, Austria, Belgium, Canada, the United Kingdom, Ireland, France, Germany, Netherlands, Denmark, Sweden, Norway, Finland, New Zealand, Singapore, and Japan. Today, companies that rely on Rokt to solve their complex ecommerce challenges include Groupon, Live Nation, Staples, Land's End, Fanatics, GoDaddy, HelloFresh, and Vistaprint.

Lessons from This Case Study

1. **Solve an important problem.** Rokt was created to solve ecommerce companies' problem that customers weren't completing purchases or buying additional products. He saw this problem firsthand at Jetstar, and he knew a solution would help ecommerce companies generate additional revenue from increased transactions.

(*continued*)

(continued)

2. **Address a large market.** Bruce recognized that maximizing ecommerce transactions would be valuable to all companies selling online, not just in the airline industry. Also, he targeted the United States because the biggest ecommerce companies were there. Notably, Rokt secured its first investors to fund its U.S. expansion because of the huge upside potential of the move.
3. **Commit fully to U.S. entry.** After proving the Rokt product and securing funding, Bruce came to the United States to build the company's U.S. business. He said, "I find a lot of entrepreneurs try to build a U.S. business remotely. And it's very hard. If you want to take a market seriously, you have to put yourself in it." The work, he said, requires "absolute commitment."
4. **Hire local talent.** While Rokt did bring a few Australians to the United States who knew the product well, most of the people hired were locals from diverse backgrounds. This local talent was more attuned to the pace of U.S. business, and they connected most easily with U.S. clients and prospects.

Notes

1. News Release, "Gross Domestic Product, Corporate Profits, and GDP by Industry, Fourth Quarter and Year 2021," U.S. Government's Bureau of Economic Analysis, March 30, 2022, www.bea.gov/news/2022/gross-domestic-product-third-estimate-corporate-profits-and-gdp-industry-fourth-quarter
2. Kieran Corcoran, "California's economy is now the 5th-biggest in the world, and has overtaken the United Kingdom," Business Insider, May 5, 2018, www.businessinsider.com/california-economy-ranks-5th-in-the-world-beating-the-uk-2018-5
3. "Why NYC," New York City Economic Development Corporation, Accessed April 24, 2022, edc.nyc/why-nyc

4. Joe White, "How and when to raise venture capital from Silicon Valley—for European and Asian startups," Medium, August 1, 2019, medium.com/entrepreneur-first/how-and-when-to-raise-venture-capital-from-silicon-valley-for-european-and-asian-startups-dd27037c1d1b
5. U.S. Census Bureau, 2022, Accessed December 4, 2021, data.census.gov/cedsci/profile?q=United%20States&g=0100000US
6. "Wage gains for low earners have helped sustain America's economic expansion," *The Economist*, February 15, 2020, www-economist-com.ezproxy.cul.columbia.edu/finance-and-economics/2020/02/13/wage-gains-for-low-earners-have-helped-sustain-americas-economic-expansion
7. Ruchir Sharma, "The Comeback Nation," Foreign Affairs, April 16, 2020, www.foreignaffairs.com/articles/united-states/2020-03-31/comeback-nation
8. Ibid.
9. Gwynn Guilford and Sarah Chaney Cambon, "The Economic Recovery Is Here. It's Unlike Anything You've Seen," *Wall Street Journal*, June 2, 2021,www.wsj.com/articles/the-economic-recovery-is-here-rebound-jobs-stock-market-unemployment-biden-aid-package-11622642152
10. Paolo Astone, "Bailouts for start-ups 'vital for recovery'," FDI Intelligence, May 13, 2020, www.fdiintelligence.com/article/77701
11. "Why Invest: World's Largest Market," SelectUSA, Accessed April 05, 2021, www.selectusa.gov/largest-market
12. FRED Economic Data, "Disposable Personal Income: Per capita: Current dollars," Federal Reserve Bank of St. Louis, June 25, 2021, fred.stlouisfed.org/series/A229RC0
13. "Distribution of Household Wealth in the U.S. since 1989," Board of Governors of the Federal Reserve System, accessed April 24, 2022, www.federalreserve.gov/releases/z1/dataviz/dfa/distribute/chart/#range:2005.4,2020.4;quarter:125;series:Net%20worth;demographic:networth;population:1,3,5,7;units:shares
14. "Supermarket Facts," FMI Food Industry Assoc., Accessed July 05, 2021, www.fmi.org/our-research/supermarket-facts
15. U.S. Census Bureau, 2022, Accessed December 4, 2021, data.census.gov/cedsci/profile?q=United%20States&g=0100000US
16. "Expanding to the US," Index Ventures, Accessed April 3, 2021, www.indexventures.com/us-expansion/changing-landscapes
17. A. Bartels, "US Tech Market Outlook For 2021 And 2022," Forrester Research Inc., April 26, 2021
18. Interview with Sofia "Puff" Story, co-founder of 3 Sided Cube, on January 25, 2021

19. Tim Sullivan, "Blitzscaling," *Harvard Business Review*, February 9, 2018, hbr.org/2016/04/blitzscaling
20. Sean Conor, "Democrats Are Now the Pro-Business Party," Bloomberg.com, January 12, 2021, www.bloomberg.com/opinion/articles/2021-01-12/democrats-are-now-the-pro-business-party
21. Kelsey Mays, "Cars.com 2018 American-Made Index: What's the Most American Car?" Cars.com, June 21, 2018, www.cars.com/articles/cars-com-2018-american-made-index-whats-the-most-american-car-1420700348632
22. "National FDI Data," Global Business Alliance, December 2, 2021, globalbusiness.org/factsheet/national-fdi-data
23. World Bank, "Doing Business 2020; Comparing Business Regulations in 190 Economies," World Bank. 2020. DOI:10.1596/978-1-4648-1440-2.
24. "The Best Countries to Start a Business," *U.S. News & World Report*, Accessed April 24, 2022, www.usnews.com/news/best-countries/best-countries-to-start-a-business
25. Ruchir Sharma, "The Comeback Nation," Foreign Affairs, April 16, 2020, www.foreignaffairs.com/articles/united-states/2020-03-31/comeback-nation
26. "PwC/CB Insights MoneyTree™ Report Q4, 2020, Accessed June 21, 2021, www.pwc.com/us/en/industries/tmt/technology/moneytree.html
27. "U.S. News Announces 2022 Best Global Universities Ranking," *U.S. News and World Report*, October 26, 2021, www.usnews.com/info/blogs/press-room/articles/2021-10-26/us-news-announces-2022-best-global-universities-rankings
28. David Teten, "Why International Startups are Attracting U.S. Venture Capitalists," Financial Poise, January 5, 2021, www.financialpoise.com/international-startups-attracting-us-venture-capitalists-2
29. Hannah Hartig, "Openness to foreigners essential to U.S. identity, say most Americans," Pew Research Center, May 30, 2020, www.pewresearch.org/fact-tank/2018/10/09/most-americans-view-openness-to-foreigners-as-essential-to-who-we-are-as-a-nation
30. "Cultural Trends 2019, Sparks & Honey. January 2019, www.sparksandhoney.com/reports-list/2019-trends
31. Sundiatu Dixon-Fyle, et al., "Diversity Wins: How inclusion matters," McKinsey & Co., May 19, 2020, www.mckinsey.com/featured-insights/diversity-and-inclusion/diversity-wins-how-inclusion-matters
32. Interview with Christian Chemaly, founder and CEO of Polar Stock, on March 1, 2021
33. Interview with Scott Weir, founder and CEO of Pillow Partners, on September 29, 2021
34. Interview with Sree Sivanandan, CEO of Networkonomy, on February 11, 2021

35. Harry J. Sapienza, et al., "A capabilities perspective on the effects of early internationalization on firm survival and growth," *Academy of Management Review*, Vol. 31, No. 4, October, 2006, pp. 914–933
36. Growth Market Reports, "Global E-commerce Software Market Expected to Reach USD 20.4 Billion by 2028 with a CAGR of 16.1%," PR Newswire, May, 2021, www.prnewswire.com/news-releases/global-e-commerce-software-market-expected-to-reach-usd-20-4-billion-by-2028--with-a-cagr-of-16-1---growth-market-reports-301292492.html
37. Angela Guido, "Is the Paradox of Choice Hurting Your Website?" MSN, June 12, 2021, www.msn.com/en-us/news/other/is-the-paradox-of-choice-hurting-your-website/ar-AAKX7NP
38. Interview with Bruce Buchanan, CEO of Rokt, on March 23, 2021
39. Sahil Patel, "E-Commerce Marketing Firm Rokt Raises $80 Million," *Wall Street Journal*, October 22, 2020, www.wsj.com/articles/e-commerce-marketing-tech-firm-rokt-raises-80-million-11603314950
40. Ellen Glover, "Rokt Scores $325M Tiger Global-led Funding as It Approaches $2B Valuation," Built In NYC, December 16, 2021, www.builtinnyc.com/2021/12/16/rokt-raises-325m-series-e-2b-valuation-hiring-marketing

3

Land of Dreams

Hamdi Ulukaya arrived in the United States with $3,000, barely able to speak English. After some success running a feta cheese company, Hamdi received a Small Business Association loan from the U.S. government to buy a bankrupt dairy factory in a small town in northern New York that reminded him of the farming villages in Eastern Turkey. Within five years his Chobani brand became the top-selling yogurt in America, with sales of $460 million.[1]

> "This magic that still exists in this country, this cannot be taught to someone," Hamdi said in an interview with the *New York Times*. "This cannot be implemented by the political system. Someone as strange as me can come to upstate New York and say: 'You know what? I can bring that yogurt factory back.' There's this unexplainable thing in the air that this country has."[2]

To be sure, the United States is a good place to seek, as Hamdi did, the fulfillment of your personal goals and dreams for your family. But several people have asked me: "How much truth is there—really—to the American success stories depicted in movies, books, and television shows? Are the many opportunities in the United States really available to me and my family?"

The answer is, "It depends." Pursuing the American Dream isn't for everyone. Generally, the Dream isn't for people who are timid, faint-hearted, or easily discouraged. Achieving the Dream requires hard work, perseverance, resilience, and a bit of luck. And the opportunities available—although abundant—aren't always distributed equally: not everyone who arrives on U.S. shores, even with the best of ideas, intentions, and motivation, will succeed. As I tell my students, "These dreams are not for the sleepy."

Yet many people do achieve their dreams here. As Roger Bennett, British-born broadcaster and filmmaker wrote, "Looking on from across the ocean, the United States appeared to me a beacon of such courage, tenacity, and wonder that it changed everything I thought was possible about the world and gave me the confidence to chase those possibilities with the passion Tracy Chapman sang about fast cars."[3]

In this chapter, we'll explore stories of fulfilled American Dreams, including those of three immigrants from France, India, and Mexico. I'll share my American Dream story, too. But first, let's look at how the idea of the Dream itself originated, how it transformed, and what it means for Americans today.

The American Dream

People around the world have heard stories of the American Dream, of immigrants who started from humble beginnings and later attained positions of great wealth and fame. They've heard tales of entrepreneurs, musicians, athletes, and actors who've come to the United States and skyrocketed to fame.

In American culture, the idea of the American Dream is a familiar theme. Our movies, children's books, and novels often end with the main character achieving a dream life of luxury, leisure, and happiness. This version has been told many times, no better than in the high-grossing animated film *An American Tail*, co-produced by Stephen Spielberg. In it, Fievel the mouse moves his family from Russia to the United States for a better life. They'd heard rumors the streets were filled with cheese and there were no cats. Needless to say, while the Mousekewitz family found many of those rumors untrue, over the course of the 80-minute movie the family discovered a fulfilling life in America.

While doing research for this book, I asked more than 100 people: "Why do you want to come to the United States?" At least 75 percent mentioned the American Dream, and I was surprised by what seemed to be a universal knowledge and belief in this concept of possibilities. When I probed further, many said they'd dreamed of living in the United States since they were children.

Pierre Gervois, a French-born entrepreneur and filmmaker whom you'll read more about later in this chapter, told me that from an early age, he became fascinated with the United States through watching movies.

"I dreamed of living in America when I was at my grandparents' home, watching a John Wayne western movie or a Clint Eastwood movie," he said. "And now today I'm making movies about the United States!" Pierre was emphatic about his reason for moving to the United States. "It's not to make money. It's not for the sake of being an entrepreneur. It's not to sell goods or services. It's the American Dream." (See Pierre's story and those of two other immigrants in the case studies later in this chapter.)

> "With hope and hard work anyone can achieve great things in America," explained Dr. Kenneth Uwajeh, executive director of the Healthy Mind Foundation Nigeria, who started a mental health clinic in Maryland. "And information, too. You need good information and advice to get things done here."

When Did the Dream Begin?

The idiom "American Dream" became a catchphrase in 1931 when James Truslow Adams featured it in his bestselling book, *The Epic of America*. He wrote, "The American dream is the belief that anyone, regardless of where they were born or what class they were born into, can attain their own version of success in a society in which upward mobility is possible for everyone. The American dream is believed to be achieved through sacrifice, risk-taking, and hard work, rather than by chance."[4]

At the time, the country was in an economic depression following the stock market crash of 1929. Half of U.S. banks failed, and unemployment was at 30 percent. James T. believed the country had forgotten its foundational principle, promised in the Declaration of Independence, that all people could achieve life, liberty, and the pursuit of happiness. He wrote *The Epic of America* to inspire people to dream once again, and he wanted to remind people that the United States was different from England and the rest of Europe, where upward mobility was limited by the family and place in society where one was born. Comically, James T. wanted to title the book *The American Dream*, but the publisher didn't think people would spend $3.50 for a book about a dream.[5]

James T. also commented on the country's obsession with material things, which had reached a new level during the "Roaring 1920s." He felt that Americans were obsessed with money and mass consumerism, since many people could afford to buy automobiles and live a lavish lifestyle. Reflecting on the American Dream, he wrote: "It is not a dream of motor cars and high wages merely, but a dream of a social order in which each man and each woman shall be able to attain to the fullest stature of which they are innately capable, and be recognized by others for what they are, regardless of the fortuitous circumstances of birth or position."

The essence of James T.'s vision of the American Dream was the idea that every person in the United States has the opportunity to achieve their personal goals.[6] And this idea of opportunity for personal fulfillment for all citizens was documented in our Declaration of Independence and Bill of Rights.

The American Dream Today

Research shows that 70 percent of Americans believe the American Dream is achievable.[7] And 36 percent of U.S. adults report their families have achieved the American Dream, with another 46 percent saying they are "on their way" to achieving it.[8] Yet, there is no consensus on what the American Dream is.

The American Dream is often portrayed in our entertainment media as a sole focus on acquiring tremendous wealth and material things. After all, Madonna sang about being a "material girl." And a popular TV special was called "Who Wants to Marry a Multi-Millionaire?" with several spin-off series. And let's not forget the movie *Jerry Maguire*, in which Cuba Gooding, Jr.'s character told Jerry, played by Tom Cruise, to "Show me the money!"

Although endless material wealth is some people's dream, that idea is more theater than reality. A truer picture is that America is a land of dreams where anything is possible—which might or might not include huge financial success. In fact, many people measure the rewards of their dreams in nonmonetary terms, such as achieving freedom from their countries' political restrictions or finding work that makes a positive impact on the world.

This view was confirmed by a Pew Research Center study that found the American Dream has different meaning for different people. The "freedom of choice in how to live" was the most important to 77 percent in their view of the American Dream. It was followed by "having a good family life" (70 percent) and being "able to retire comfortably" (60 percent). Despite the perception of American "bling" culture, only 11 percent said that becoming wealthy was the key to their view of the American Dream.[9]

One reason for Americans' widespread optimism is that they feel they are in control of their destiny. That view aligns with the country's Puritan origins and an ethic that attributes success to how hard people work. In an earlier Pew Research Study that was conducted in 44 countries, 57 percent of U.S. citizens <u>disagreed</u> with the statement "Success in life is pretty much determined by forces outside our control." This was higher than most other nations and far above the median of 38 percent for all countries.[10]

My American Dream

I'm one of the 36 percent of U.S. citizens who believe they have achieved and are living their American Dream. What's more, as I recounted in this book's introduction, I'm also a product of the American Dream: My ancestors immigrated to the United States around the turn of the 20th century, seeking a better life than the one they had in Eastern Europe.

But I also feel extremely grateful and lucky regarding the circumstances of my life today. I'm married to a wonderful person, live in a comfortable house, enjoy my work, and have two creative and talented children. I've also had some happy successes in my career. I owe much of that success to my upbringing in a supportive environment and the many opportunities handed to me, which not every American child experiences.

I grew up surrounded by books, newspapers, and magazines. My mother was a public school librarian, and she regularly brought home the latest books for my brother and me. My father read five newspapers: *Boston Globe*, *New York Times*, *Wall Street Journal*, *Christian Science Monitor*, and *Jewish Advocate*. Our family also subscribed to *Newsweek*, *People*, *Sports Illustrated*, and *U.S. News & World Report*. You could say we were "news junkies."

As a teenager, I fulfilled an early dream of writing for a newspaper in Brookline, Massachusetts. Like many American Dreamers around the world, I'd been highly influenced from watching movies. I became attracted to journalism after viewing "All the President's Men"—the story of two journalists, Bob Woodward and Carl Bernstein, who uncovered the Watergate scandal that led to Richard Nixon's resignation as U.S. President. Later, after I became an editor of the high school newspaper, *The Brookline Sagamore*, I achieved another dream when it won a Gold medal from Columbia University's School of Journalism for being one of the best high school newspapers in the country.

The Sagamore's faculty adviser, Sandy Fowler, convinced me to study something other than journalism in college, though, believing that the best journalists become experts in a subject, such as science or music, and then find publications where they can write about it. I chose the subject of business and enrolled at the University of Michigan in Ann Arbor, which had both an excellent student newspaper and business school.

During college, I had a summer job at *The Boston Globe* newspaper. Mostly it was calling and interviewing people over the telephone. There was a close political race for governor of Massachusetts, and the Globe wanted to get a pulse on voters' sentiment. The work also included market research for local advertisers. It was extremely boring and nothing like the glamour of Woodward and Bernstein. I never got to write and publish a single sentence.

After college, I worked in New York City with Backer & Spielvogel Advertising. The agency, which later was absorbed by Saatchi & Saatchi, produced memorable campaigns for brands such as Miller Lite, Sony, Wendy's, and Campbell's Soup. We also introduced Hyundai into the United States, which I'll tell you about in Chapter 11. Over the next two decades, I worked in management roles for several notable companies, including BIC, Chinet, Digitas, Pitney Bowes, and Snapple Beverages.

Through the years, however, I still had one major unfulfilled dream: writing and publishing a book. Then, in 2014, I stumbled happily into teaching and consulting. That work placed me on a path to writing this—my first book—and finally fulfilling an ultimate dream.

Fulfilling Your Dream

Now that I've told you my American Dream story, let's focus on turning your dreams into reality. As promised from the book's subtitle, I want to help you successfully enter and scale your business in U.S. markets. The first step, which is the subject of the next chapter, is to create a strategic plan that, if effectively executed, will achieve your stated goals and measurable objectives.

But first, let's look at three stories of people who came to the United States in search of their American Dream.

Case Study: Three American Dreams

The American Dream has drawn people from around the world to the United States. Many believe that the United States is a place where, with hard work, determination, and a little luck, anyone can achieve financial prosperity and a good life. But the truth is that each person who comes to the United States has their own story and reasons.

Jordi Muñoz (Mexico)

As a boy in Mexico, Jordi Muñoz loved science and dreamed of being a pilot. At the age of 20, he moved to Southern California with his soon-to-be wife to pursue a career in engineering. But he first needed the necessary visa to get a job. During seven months of waiting for a visa, Jordi kept busy surfing the Internet and writing software. He later said, "I was bored a lot at home, so I started playing with chips and controllers; I spent hours experimenting with the code, browsing, and reading on the computer."[11]

Jordi became fascinated with the Unmanned Aerial Vehicle (UAV) industry, which was just starting to take off. Essentially, a UAV, also known as a drone, is a remote-controlled plane with an attached camera for taking aerial photographs and videos. He designed and built his first drone in 2007, which used circuitry found in a Nintendo Wii remote control to create an autopilot system. Later he repurposed an electric toaster into a reflow oven to attach microchips to circuit boards to create a more advanced prototype. From his apartment near Los Angeles, Jordi designed and created parts for drones, which he sold on the Internet.

During this protype-building time, Jordi became active in the do-it-yourself (DIY) drone online community. There he shared stories about his undertakings and posted videos of his drones in flight. His posts caught the attention of Chris Anderson, editor-in-chief of *Wired* magazine who wrote about technology trends. After some online correspondence, Chris sent Jordi $500 to build and sell several dozen prototypes. It worked splendidly, and Chris continued to advise Jordi through email and telephone. The business started growing really fast, and Jordi knew that he needed to bring in experienced people to help with the business operations and management.

In 2009, Jordi and Chris founded 3D Robotics, with headquarters in Berkeley, California. Chris was the chief executive officer (CEO), and Jordi was the chief technology officer (CTO) overseeing the engineering center in San Diego, California. By 2012, the company generated $10 million in revenue. By the end of 2014, 3D Robotics employed more than 350 people in three U.S. and one Mexican locations.[12] (3D Robotics later downsized in 2016 when dozens of Chinese competitors entered the market with low-cost products. But that's a different story.)

While he didn't achieve his original dream of becoming a pilot, Jordi achieved great heights. In 2012, he was honored by the *Massachusetts Institute of Technology Review* for his innovation in computer and electronics hardware. When asked about the United States and his personal dream, Jordi said, "It is really a land of opportunities. It doesn't matter what is your background. If you work hard, you do the right thing, and you're honest, you can always do whatever you want United States." He noted, however, that "you must be very persistent. You must keep trying, over and over again and try to reach your goal. Even if you don't reach your goal, the path that you follow to get there may take you to something better."[13]

(*continued*)

(continued)

Pooja Mahajan (India)

Pooja Mahajan moved to the United States from India in 2010 to pursue a master's degree in environmental engineering at Clemson University. Many of her Indian friends had chosen to study engineering or medicine at home, but she took a more courageous path to pursue a bigger dream. Pooja said, "What really attracted me to this country was the idea of the American Dream—that glamorous dream of having a six-figure salary, a luxurious car, a big house, and a whole lot more."[14] Even though she had to take out a $30,000 personal loan, she felt it was a small price for a chance at reaching her dream.

At Clemson, Pooja met and later married a fellow student. In her classes, she received high grades and worked as an unpaid research assistant. Her master's thesis—on designing and modeling a wind-powered reverse osmosis desalination system using an air-pressure energy storage mechanism—received international recognition.

But after graduation, Pooja had a difficult time finding a job. Companies were reluctant to hire recent graduates without U.S. citizenship. One reason is that some employers resist having to collect data and coordinate with lawyers and government agencies. But the main reason for some companies' reluctance is that they must sponsor any noncitizens for an employment visa, in most cases an H-1B. Since there are always more applicants than available H-1B visas, applicants are put into a lottery. Many employers don't want risk losing a trained worker after a couple of years if in the end they aren't selected in the lottery. (Chapter 10 provides an overview of the U.S. visa system.)

After 15 months of job hunting and hundreds of interviews, Pooja landed a job with an engineering firm. They offered to sponsor her for a visa, too. It did require her to move to a different city, which took her away from her husband during the week. Nonetheless, she took the job to get started on her career.

From the start, Pooja found the work environment demeaning and unpleasant. Colleagues and her boss mocked her for being a woman in a man's engineering world. Several times she wanted to quit and return home. After two years, she was fired without prior warning. Pooja felt rejected by the United States, and she questioned the dream it promised, wondering if it had been worth taking the risk of coming to America.

And yet, Pooja soon decided she wasn't ready to give up on the United States. She realized she'd been measuring the success in financial terms and not personal goals and choices. "I realized the American dream is not a package deal of having a job, a car, and a house. It is about making intentional choices for yourself and taking ownership of those choices. Being close to my family, waiting for the right job opportunity, and working at a company that respected me was some of the choices I made since losing my job."[15]

Not long after making that decision, Pooja landed a job with AECOM, a highly respected engineering and design company. They sponsored her, and she received a visa. After two years, AECOM transferred her to their Los Angeles headquarters, where she is managing multiple important projects. Happily, she said, "Today I'm living the American Dream of my choices."

Pierre Gervois (France)

Pierre Gervois is an artist, author, teacher, and entrepreneur. He grew up in a conservative, traditional French family in Paris. When Pierre told his parents that he

(*continued*)

(continued)

wanted to study modern art, they insisted he pursue a more predictable career in business, law, or engineering. He followed their wishes, earning a master's degree in political science and constitutional law at Institut d'Etudes Politiques de Paris. Unknown to them, though, during those years he also created 500 paintings and drawings.

After earning his degree, Pierre worked in international economic relations for the French government, with a specialization on China. Eventually, he became the head of the Chinese desk at the National Federation of Chambers of Commerce and Industry. In 2004, he joined an investment firm to expand their business in China, specifically in the tourism and hospitality sector.

With his insight into the growing Chinese tourism market, Pierre moved to Shanghai in 2007 to start a media company, China Elite Focus Limited, which published luxury travel magazines for newly affluent Chinese. The firm also created digital marketing campaigns for luxury brands, including Piaget and Van Cleef & Arpels, and upscale hotels, such as the Ritz.

Since the United States was both the top destination for Chinese tourists and the firm's greatest source of revenue, Pierre decided to move to New York in 2013. However, after five profitable years, the tourism market shifted. Luxury hotels and shops became overrun with Chinese tourists who freely spent money on their goods, and they didn't feel the need to pay for advertising and marketing services to attract business. One luxury retailer who ended a contract with Pierre told him that the plentiful Chinese tourists made Pierre's services obsolete.

China Elite Focus closed in December 2017. Rather than head back to France, Pierre chose to stay in the United States and try to find a new source of income.

Faced with rising debt and few job opportunities in the publishing industry, Pierre decided to start a new venture that leveraged his knowledge of the tourism business, media creation, and passion for art. Pierre and his wife, Christelle Bois, an accomplished photographer, started a film production company to produce films about art in America. The new venture, appropriately called Legit Productions, launched in January 2019. About his new path, Pierre said, "Only in America can you reinvent yourself."[16]

As mentioned earlier in this chapter, as a child in France, Pierre had become fascinated with the United States through the old western movies he watched with his grandparents. Now he had the chance to make movies himself, in America. Despite never having produced a film before, Pierre was able to convince 10 cities to co-produce a documentary film that featured their art scene. Their film, titled AmericArt 2019, was selected for seven film festivals and released to the public on Amazon Prime Video in June 2020. Based on this success, Pierre then produced a documentary series titled *The Story of Art in America* that was released in early 2020. It explores the country's diverse arts communities from painting to poetry, music to sculpture, and pottery to theater and dance. He said they want to show how art is and always will be an essential part of America's social fabric. Pierre went on to film a second season in 2022.

In addition to his entrepreneurial venture, Pierre rekindled his passion for art. With downtime during the 2020 pandemic, he created a website to show his paintings, drawings, and digital artwork. Within six weeks, he sold five pieces. The website also caught the attention of a New York City art gallery that wanted to exhibit his work.

(*continued*)

(*continued*)

Today Pierre not only produces movies and creates art, he also is raising a family and teaching at a major U.S. university. He doesn't hesitate to say that he's living his American Dream. "I feel like I have this complete freedom to be exactly the person I want to be," he says, "and in all directions!"

Lessons from These Case Studies

1. **Choose your American Dream.** Each of these three people had a different goal and dream. Jordi dreamed of flying planes, Pierre dreamed of making movies, and Pooja discovered her dream of being in control of her destiny. In the United States, there are many kinds of dreams that can be pursued.
2. **The United States welcomes talent.** Jordi, Pierre, and Pooja all possess skills and talents that are recognized and wanted in the United States, by either employers, investors, or consumers. Although each of their paths met challenges and delays, in the end they were welcomed in this country.
3. **Be persistent and flexible.** Each of these people met obstacles and delays. Pooja nearly gave up and went back to her home country. It takes strength and a good support network to be persistent and keep trying. It also takes being flexible and adjusting to the opportunities that present themselves.
4. **Importance of visa advice.** The U.S. immigration system can be confusing and frustratingly slow. It requires good advice from knowledgeable immigration professionals and lawyers, support from employers, plus a bit of luck.

Notes

1. Mamta Badkar, "Trendy Greek Yogurt Chobani is Officially the Top Selling Brand in America," Business Insider, Oct. 8, 2011, www.businessinsider.com/americas-favorite-yogurt-2011-10
2. David Gelles, "Hamdi Ulukaya of Chobani Talks Greek Yogurt and the American Dream," *The New York Times*, August 24, 2018, www.nytimes.com/2018/08/24/business/hamdi-ulukaya-chobani-corner-office.html
3. Roger Bennett, *(Re)born in the USA* (New York: Harper Collins, 2021), p. 20
4. *James Truslow Adams papers, 1918–1949* (New York: Columbia University Library), Accessed April 12, 2021, www.columbia.edu/cu/lweb/archival/collections/ldpd_4078384
5. Allan Nevins, *James Truslow Adams, Historian of the American Dream*, (Chicago, Il.: University of Illinois Press, 1968) p. 296
6. Tom Nicholas and David Chen, The American Dream in History, *Harvard Business Review*, April 27, 2022
7. Mohamid Younis, "Most Americans See American Dream as Achievable," Gallup, July 17, 2019, news.gallup.com/poll/260741/americans-american-dream-achievable.aspx
8. Samantha Smith, "Most Think the 'American dream' is Within Reach for Them," Pew Research Center (blog), Accessed May 8, 2022, www.pewresearch.org/fact-tank/2017/10/31/most-think-the-american-dream-is-within-reach-for-them
9. A.W. Geiger, "How Americans See Their Country and Their Democracy," Pew Research Center, July 4, 2018, www.pewresearch.org/fact-tank/2018/07/04/how-americans-see-their-country-and-their-democracy
10. George Goa, "How Americans Stand Out", Pew Research Center, May 12, 2015, www.pewresearch.org/fact-tank/2015/03/12/how-do-americans-stand-out-from-the-rest-of-the-world
11. Chris Anderson, "Congrats to Jordi: One of MIT Technology Review's Top Entrepreneurs Under 35," DIY Drones, May 14, 2012, diydrones.com/profiles/blogs/congrats-to-jordi-one-of-mit-technology-review-s-top-entrepreneur
12. Regan Morris, "The Mexican immigrant who set up a global drone firm," BBC News, February 23, 2015, www.bbc.com/news/business-31356080
13. Ibid.
14. Pooja Mahajan, "Living the American Dream," TEDX Greenville, Accessed May 5, 2022, tedxgreenville.com/portfolio/pooja-mahajan
15. Ibid.
16. Conversation with Pierre Gervois, founder and CEO of Legit Productions, on February 22, 2021

4

Plan for Success

Former U.S. President Dwight Eisenhower once said, "In preparing for battle I have always found that plans are useless, but planning is indispensable."[1] While pursuing the American Dream isn't exactly a battle, you will want to plan for your success. Companies always do such planning. When making critical business decisions on complex issues, companies establish clear goals to guide their deliberations. This planning process is important because you need to be prepared for whatever might come up, understanding that you have no way of reliably knowing what actually will happen. Therefore, you'll want to establish realistic goals, measurable objectives, and a comprehensive Go-to-U.S. market strategy.

This chapter focuses on strategy and planning for business success, moving from hopes and dreams (as covered in the previous chapter) to an actionable strategy for achieving them. It includes a spotlight on a Canadian company that decided to expand into the United States, and I'll share what's needed to make actionable strategic goals. We'll also examine the kinds of strategies that small and early-stage businesses can develop, and we'll look at the qualities that characterize successful companies.

> "I see too many companies fail because they don't have a clear plan," says Federico Tozzi, executive director of the Italy-America Chamber of Commerce. "They have no strategy. They think, we'll figure it out when we get there."[2]

First, however, let's begin with a framework you can use for your own strategic planning process. Strategic planning is especially important for international companies trying to enter and scale in U.S. markets, and a framework is a way to organize and evaluate the pieces of the strategy. Think of the framework as a lens or window to view the big picture and the elements. The framework will help you translate your dreams into clear goals and measurable objectives. It will help you determine where to enter and the best way to compete. If you are already doing business in the United States, you'll probably still want to strengthen your strategic plans to better attract customers, employees, and investors. In all cases, the strategic planning process will help prepare you for potential obstacles and opportunities in highly competitive and fast-paced U.S. markets.

Strategic Framework

There are many frameworks and templates for strategic business plans. My favorite was created by A.G. Lafley and Roger Martin, published in the 2013 book *Playing to Win*. I've taught dozens of business strategy courses at several universities using this framework. It has led to hundreds of students creating excellent strategic plans based on solid thinking, research, and analysis.

Despite the authors' corporate backgrounds—Lafley was the chief executive officer and chairman of Procter & Gamble, and Martin was dean of University of Toronto's Rotman School of Management—the framework works well for entrepreneurs, too. While startups often discover their business strategies through an iterative test-and-learn approach, they still need a strategic plan to pitch investors and potential partners.

Lafley and Martin's framework is based on their view that strategy is a set of choices that position the organization or brand in a way that creates an advantage and superior value over the competition.[3] To make strategic choices, their framework requires you to answer five essential questions.

- What is your winning aspiration?
- Where will you play?
- How will you win?
- What capabilities must be in place?
- What management systems are required?

Keep in mind when creating your strategic plans that these questions are interrelated. Rather than answering them in a linear step process, it's best to work through them in an iterative way—that is, you'll likely need to return to each question more than once when developing your strategic framework.

What Is Your Winning Aspiration?

The first step is determining your goal or winning aspiration for your U.S. business. Is your goal to become a global player and not just a one-country business? Maybe it's to prove your product is the best so you can be the global industry leader. There is no right answer. Every organization and every situation are different, so every organization should have their own goal: their own winning aspiration.

Since the concept of winning is abstract, Lafley and Martin say it needs to be translated into defined aspirations. In their model, aspirations are statements about an ideal future.[4] For example, P&G's aspiration for its Olay brand was to create sustainable competitive advantage, superior value for consumers, and superior financial returns. Rokt's winning aspiration, as shown in the Chapter 2 case study, was to be the global leader in ecommerce software.

If your goal is simply to "make money," that is not a winning aspiration. Making money is a result of executing a strong strategic plan. Winning aspirations should motivate and inspire people in your organization. Winning aspirations can be lofty and far-reaching, but they should be attainable and realistic. The goals should give people a clear idea of what success looks like. For example, one Danish company scaled up its operations by entering the United States with a winning aspiration: reducing food waste in the world to improve lives and reduce global warming. (See "Case Study: Too Good to Go" at the end of this chapter.)

Where to Play?

If you're reading this book, you're probably thinking of entering and/or expanding in U.S. markets. However, you need to be more specific. The U.S. marketplace is too big and too diverse to try to compete everywhere. There are more than 330 million people living in 3.8 million square miles (9.1 million square kilometers). Among them there are countless submarkets with more ethnic groups than any other country. There are 637 languages spoken in New York City alone![5]

Where on the U.S. map should you try to enter? What geographic locations? It could be one city, one region, or multiple places. This decision will set the stage for your strategies around things such as marketing, human resources, and factory or office location. The decision of geography is particularly important for international companies that need to establish a U.S. presence and deal with local taxes, regulations, and employment practices.

Certainly, which customers you decide to target is a crucial component of your where-to-play decision. No company or brand can be all things to all people, so you need to select which consumer market segment you want to serve. If you're selling a business-to-business (B2B) product, what businesses and functional departments will your salespeople be calling on? A producer of heart-rate monitoring devices, for instance, might target the information technology (IT) department of hospitals or the cardiologists who operate there.

Moreover, where-to-play decisions often include the product categories in which you choose to compete. For example, will your product be a high-priced product in the luxury category of goods, or will it be sold at a low price point in the economy segment of the market? Also, where will your product fall in the vertical stage, or stages, of the production and marketing chain?

It could be the manufacturing stage or the distribution and selling stages. For B2B products, it's often easier for international companies to sell a component to an established U.S. company to combine into a total solution—rather than selling individual pieces or ingredients.

Where-to-play decisions also include how you will reach and communicate with prospects and customers. Will it be through digital channels or in-person at conferences and events? Lastly, where will people buy your product? Will it be on your website, on Amazon or another online marketplace, or in a physical store? (See also Chapter 6, which focuses on decision-making around U.S. locations and other places to play.)

How to Win?

How-to-win decisions define the method that your organization, or brand, will try to outperform the competition. Why will customers and business clients want to buy your product or service? Business consultants would frame the question as, "What is the value proposition?" Advertising professionals would ask, "What is the brand's promise?" Is it a better product or a lower price for acceptable quality? Is it a more convenient way to purchase the product or service?

Most U.S. markets have many competitors and options for consumers, so the value proposition needs to be strong to gain traction. Therefore, it is important to investigate the competitive landscape. Your investigation should include both companies currently offering similar products and potential competitors that could enter the market.

Be careful not to assume that you already know what U.S. customers' tastes and perception of quality might be. The notion of what is "better" or "best" may be very different in the United States than your country. The German company, Menck Fenster, discovered U.S. homeowners had vastly different requirements and needs than European homeowners. (You can read the case study on the company's expensive mistake in Chapter 5.)

Where-to-play and how-to-win decisions are often tackled together, as they are interrelated. Together they are the central pieces of the strategy. A classic example is Apple, which in 2007 won a lion's share of the U.S. smartphone market with its winning formula of sleek product design, uncompromising engineering, and sublime user experience. The Japanese company Sony used this same combination of winning attributes in 1979, when it captured the U.S. music-player market with the smartly designed and innovatively engineered Walkman.

What Capabilities Are Needed?

After determining the core strategic questions of "where to play" and "how to win," you need to assess if your organization has the necessary resources and competencies to succeed. Will your management team and staff be able to realistically deliver on this strategy for U.S. entry and expansion? If not, can these capabilities be acquired through hiring staff and consultants or business partnerships?

This question is particularly important for international companies and entrepreneurs deciding what people to hire and where they should be located. Will you need a dedicated salesforce in the United States, or will the product be sold on an ecommerce website? Will you need additional software or a website dedicated for the U.S. market? Even if your website is in English, it still needs to be "Americanized"—for example, British bakeries need to use the word *cookies* instead of *biscuits*, and they need to talk in *dollars* and *inches* not in *pounds* and *centimeters*.

These needed capabilities will drive the amount of money required to fund the operation and setup. There's even an emerging industry that specializes in providing a "soft landing" and easier path for businesses in the United States. For example, International Management Solutions (IMS) in Chicago provides tax and accounting consulting and operational support to midsize organizations mostly from foreign countries. President

Antoine Guillaud said they "enable companies to meet all the complicated regulations and tax requirements that would create major headaches for [international] companies."[6]

What Management and Support Systems Are Required?

The last essential question in the framework looks at what management and support systems will be needed. What processes and tools will you need to measure and support the strategy, both in the short and long term? This includes collecting and analyzing data that provides information to improve and refine strategies and tactics.

Another aspect of management systems is communication with employees and business partners. How will you establish and reinforce the corporate culture with your people over time? How will you onboard new employees so they have the same understanding and level of commitment to the company's vision as current team members have?

This question on management systems is often overlooked by business executives from every country, but it is especially critical for sustained growth in U.S. markets. Situations and conditions can change quickly in many U.S. markets and industries, so it's critical to monitor market dynamics, competitors, and the local team's performance.

The French company BIC has maintained strong market share in the United States with its disposable shavers, lighters, and writing instruments. For decades, it has sold hundreds of millions of pens during a short back-to-school season between June and September. This represents 40 percent of its annual sales, so the company can't afford to manufacture too few pens. But to maintain cost leadership, it also can't afford to make too many pens. Therefore, BIC invested in marketing research software systems that project consumer demand, monitor store purchases, and deliver accurate projections for manufacturing just the right quantity of pens in each of its many colors and varieties.

Spotlight: White Claw (Canada)

When Canadian businessman Anthony von Mandl wanted to expand his beverage company, he launched White Claw into the U.S. alcoholic sparkling water market. At the time in 2015, sales for this category, also known as spiked seltzers, were only $3 million[7]. Anthony thought the category had a lot of potential, as American consumers were interested in healthier and lower-calorie alcoholic beverages. It also had few serious competitors. Coors Brewing Company and Anheuser-Busch had spiked seltzer brands, but they did little to promote them because they didn't want the products cannibalizing their beer sales.

Anthony's winning aspiration was to both grow the spiked seltzer category and be the market leader. He had accomplished this feat before when his Vancouver-based wine business introduced Mike's Hard Lemonade in the late 1990s. That brand practically invented the ready-to-drink alcoholic beverage category, which was an attractive alternative to beer.

White Claw's how-to-win strategy was closely linked to its decision of "where to play." It chose a narrowly defined market segment and then crafted compelling brand and marketing messages that resonated with that audience. In addition, the product design and packaging appealed to that market segment.

Its key where-to-play decision was targeting Millennials, adults 25–40 years old. The company recognized that Millennials didn't relate to beer companies' marketing and portrayal of men and women. As Sanjiv Gajiwala, vice president of marketing for White Claw, explained, "It wasn't a world where guys got together in a basement and drank beer and women were off doing something else, drinking with their girlfriends," Gajiwala said. "Whatever we put out creatively and how we positioned the brand really reflects that everyone hangs out together all the time."[8]

Another where-to-play decision was to sell the product primarily in consumer outlets such as supermarkets and convenience stores. It could have chosen restaurants and bars, known in the industry as the *on-premise market*, but it wanted to leverage the company's sales and distribution expertise with Mike's

Hard Lemonade. In addition, the product packaging reinforced its "healthier alternative to beer" positioning that appealed to both women and men. It also chose to launch White Claw in slimmer, taller cans than traditional beer cans to further differentiate the brand from the competition.

Anthony's team was extremely capable of executing White Claw's Go-to-U.S. strategy. They had a strong sales and marketing organization that had been developed and tested with Mike's Hard Lemonade. They had the management and operations experience in the beverage industry. They also knew how to monitor consumer trends and track the brand's sales performance in each channel of distribution. This proved very valuable when it came to efficiently manufacturing a product to meet consumer and retailer demands.

As a result, White Claw was a runaway success. According to industry data, the brand's sales quadrupled from $155 million in 2018 to $627 million in 2019.[9] Anthony did pretty well, too. Forbes reported that his beverage business in the United States "will deliver close to $4 billion in revenue in 2020." The publication also report that Anthony von Mandl is personally worth $8.7 billion.[10]

SMART Objectives

Once you've determined your winning aspiration, the next step is turning this goal into specific objectives for your strategic plan. Goals tell you where you want to be; objectives are the steps for getting there. Objectives define what you are trying to accomplish.

Objectives should be clear and concrete. In business strategy courses, we teach that objectives need to be SMART. This acronym translates to the following:

Specific
Measurable
Achievable
Relevant
Time-based

For example, let's say a Korean food company's goal is to successfully enter and establish a foothold in the U.S. market for its artisanal brand of kimchi. A SMART objective would be to achieve $10 million dollars of annual sales in U.S. grocery stores within three years of launch. That objective is *Specific* in the exact amount of annual sales it desires to achieve. It is *Measurable* from sales data gathered at retail stores. Ideally, the numerical objective will be *Achievable* if it's based on research with consumers or surveys with retail buyers. The company's objective is *Relevant* because it directly ties to its profitability and eventual survival. Finally, it is *Time-based* in that the objective clearly defines the time frame of three years.

Small Business Strategies

Small-business owners and startup founders need to be extremely strategic in their utilization of limited resources, time, and energy. Therefore, it's even more important for them to be clear and realistic about their goals and SMART objectives.

In 2015, I taught a class on entrepreneurship at Parsons School of Design in New York City. Guest speakers included entrepreneurs, investors, and lawyers from NYC's startup ecosystem. One theme was the difficulty of starting a company and the need for realistic expectations.

For example, David Greenberg, founder and CEO of Updater, told the students that starting a company was like "going through a maze where the walls keep moving." Another guest speaker, Sky Fernandes, founder of Venture University and VU Venture Partners, explained how venture capital (VC) investors evaluate deals. He said most VC firms see hundreds of pitches a year and invest in only a handful. Many top VCs won't invest in an early-stage company unless it has the potential to be a $1 billion–valued unicorn.

One student, who was South Asian, was financing his education by selling one-of-a-kind, custom wedding dresses that were designed in the United States and produced in India. It was a healthy business that was paying his education and living expenses in New York City. The student asked for my help creating a pitch deck to secure VC money. Basically, I talked him out of it. My advice was to grow his wedding dress business organically, without investors, through capital from increased sales. The problem with having investors, such as money from venture capitalists, is that you are essentially giving them a say—a level of control—in how you do business. That creates additional, often unnecessary pressure. And in the dress manufacturer's case, securing outside investors wasn't necessary. If the company was profitable, maybe with revenues of a few million dollars a year, he could have a nice life with a sizable salary to live in a comfortable home and send his children to good schools. And he wouldn't be beholden to demanding investors. Later he thanked me. He is still running the company.

Characteristics of Successful Companies

One element of Lafley and Martin's *Playing to Win* model, mentioned earlier in this chapter, focuses on business capabilities and management skills that are needed to be successful. In addition to being capable and competent in business areas, the company should also embody a cultural philosophy or mindset that will enable its people to tackle the challenges and uncertainties that will undoubtedly arise.

"[N]othing sharpens the vision or brings greater clarity to the understanding of a product's value proposition and business model than the prospect of taking it abroad," writes Doug Quackenbos, a professor at the University of South Carolina. But, he adds, "Research shows that identifying and overcoming the internal barriers to success is perhaps even more important than understanding the more easily identifiable external factors."

In a *Harvard Business Review* article, Quackenbos and his co-authors ask: "Does your company have what it takes to go global?"[11] From their decades of work with more than 100 global companies, the authors witnessed that certain internal characteristics have determined success far more than external factors.

The article identified seven characteristics that companies need to win globally. Here is the list of what the authors call "The Seven 'tudes of International Expansion":

Attitude: Prioritizes global expansion
Aptitude: Has the right knowledge and skills to succeed abroad
Magnitude: Aligns the scale and scope of the overseas opportunities with its goals and capabilities
Latitude: Adapts its marketing and sales policies and practices to the opportunity
Rectitude: Legal and ethical practices allow for overseas flexibility while maintaining corporate compliance
Exactitude: Corporate culture tolerates some financial ambiguity and market uncertainty
Fortitude: Committed to global initiatives, even in the face of setbacks.

In a research study of more than 300 international business professionals, the authors found that organizations that scored higher on these seven dimensions performed better. On average, 77 percent of respondents in winning firms agreed their company excelled across these seven dimensions.[12]

Communication and Trust

Clear, accurate, and timely communication is critical for doing business in U.S. markets. It's true for all organizations, and it's especially true when doing business in a new country. Communication is important when managing employees, and it is doubly important when managing people from different cultural backgrounds and native languages. As covered in Chapter 9 about understanding Americans, we can be very blunt and straightforward in our communications. Therefore, you shouldn't be afraid of being open and candid about expectations and any problems or questions you might have.

Sree Sivanandan is a managing partner of NetworkOnomy Ventures, a consulting firm in India that connects startup founders and C-level executives with growth opportunities. Previously, he launched AOL's operations across several Asia Pacific countries. Sree believes the most important factors for international businesspeople working with Americans are open communication and mutual trust. Trust is built through delivering on agreed expectations and shared values. He says, "It is important to play by the rules that are acceptable to the U.S. customers and partners. . . . There is an ethical framework in which you need to run a business in the United States."[13]

In the next chapter, we'll examine a crucial component that needs to be more explicitly addressed in your market entry and expansion plans. That is the element of time. But first let's look at the inspiring case study of a Danish company whose goal is to both make money and contribute to solving a serious global problem.

Case Study: Too Good to Go (Denmark)

The inspiration for Too Good to Go (TGTG) started in Copenhagen when a team of entrepreneurs asked what became of leftover food at a buffet. They learned the uneaten meals and food items were tossed in the trash. Upon further inquiry, they discovered most restaurants, caterers, and bakeries discarded uneaten food at the end of each day even if it was still fresh and edible. In fact, it's estimated that a third of all fruits, vegetables, meat, and other foods are thrown away.[14]

The entrepreneurs wondered if it was possible to utilize technology to reduce food waste and make a positive societal impact. They envisioned "a planet with zero

(*continued*)

(*continued*)

food waste is a better place to be."[15] Just in the United States, an estimated 11 percent of the population are "food insecure," meaning they lack consistent access to enough food for a healthy life.[16] In addition, food waste is estimated to be responsible for 10 percent of all CO_2 emissions contributing to global warming, according to the Intergovernmental Panel on Climate Change (IPCC) report.

TGTG was incorporated in 2015 with the goal of fighting food waste by empowering people to act. Later it earned Certified B Corporation designation, which is awarded to companies that meet high standards for social and environmental performance. The team developed a technology platform, accessed through a mobile app, that connects consumers with businesses whose products would have otherwise gone unsold and would have to be thrown away. Their business-to-consumer (B2C) marketplace enabled people to buy fresh meals and food items from restaurants, bakeries, and grocery stores—at one-third of the price. To simplify the ordering and fulfillment process, Danish consumers could then purchase a "Magic Bag" of food from each seller. Businesses eagerly signed up for the service, as it enabled them to recover sunk costs, and it introduced their business to new customers.

After proving the business model and technology in Copenhagen, the company expanded throughout Denmark and other European countries. Its model was to hire a country manager to coordinate operations with a local team. Revenue was generated from businesses paying a yearly subscription fee and from a small commission fee for each meal sold. It expanded to 14 European countries with 38,000 business partners and more than 18 million consumer users by 2019. In the process, the company claims, it saved 29 million meals and avoided more than 72,000 metric tons of greenhouse gas emissions.[17]

TGTG launched in New York City in September 2020. Within one year it had operations in 11 cities. Some adjustments needed to be made for the U.S. market, such as renaming "Magic Bags" to "Surprise Bags." By mid-2021, the company had more than 1 million U.S. app users and saved more than 7,000,000 meals from ending up in trash cans and landfills.

"The response in the U.S. market has been incredible," said Lucie Basch, French-born co-founder of TGTG and chief expansion officer. "Americans have really embraced the concept of fighting food waste while supporting local and acting sustainably in a fun way. We've seen faster growth here than in any of the European countries we've launched to date."[18]

Jonas Mallisse, VP of Global Expansion, said the culture of the company brought together a diverse group of people who shared the common goal of creating positive change. (Jonas was a country manager in Belgium and Poland before moving to NYC in 2020.) Their team of highly motivated Waste Warriors feel they are part of a community and a movement.[19]

To fund the expansion in North America, the company needed additional funding. TGTG received $31 million investment in January 2021, led by $15.4 million from Blisce, a Certified B Corporation and VC firm focused on mission-driven consumer brands and technology companies. Alexandre Mars, founder and CEO said about TGTG, "From the outset, its team has shown an impressive singular vision: that it is possible to embed social impact within the business model and generate impressive results while making a difference for people and the planet."[20]

(*continued*)

(*continued*)

In recognition of its noble goal and success in the United States and other countries, TGTG won *Fast Company*'s World Changing Ideas Award in the app category in 2021.

Lessons from This Case Study

1. **Create winning goals that inspire.** TGTG was founded on the meaningful and important vision to create a better world with less food waste. It had a clear and compelling goal that attracted consumers, business partners, employees, and investors with similar aspirations.
2. **Choose the right time to expand.** TGTG expanded to European countries after testing and proving the concept in Copenhagen. It entered the United States only after creating a strong European business, developing a solid management team, and securing the necessary funding.
3. **Decide where to play carefully.** The founders targeted urban areas, because of the concentration of food service businesses and consumers. The decision of a mobile app coincided with the rise of online shopping and smartphone adoption. Also, they chose to compete in only one section of the value chain—the online transaction marketplace—which avoided the cost and complexity of purchasing items and holding inventory.
4. **Hire people who share your vision.** People hired were from many different countries and backgrounds, but they all shared a passion for making the world better by reducing food waste. This common vision led to an impassioned workforce of Waste Warriors who opened new markets and convinced business partners and consumers to join their community.

Notes

1. "Dwight D. Eisenhower Quotes," BrainyQuote, Accessed May 8, 2022, www.brainyquote.com/quotes/dwight_d_eisenhower_164720
2. Conversation with Federico Tozzi, executive director of the Italy-America Chamber of Commerce, on February 5, 2021
3. A.G. Lafley and Roger Martin, *Playing to Win* (Boston, Massachusetts: Harvard Business Review Press, 2013), p. 3.
4. A.G. Lafley and Roger Martin, *Playing to Win* (Boston, Massachusetts: Harvard Business Review Press, 2013), p. 19
5. Kimiko de Freytas-Tamura, "Just 700 Speak This Language (50 in the Same Brooklyn Building)," *The New York Times*, January 7, 2020, www.nytimes.com/2020/01/07/nyregion/rare-languages-seke-vlashki-wakhi.html
6. Conversation with Antoine Guillaud, president of International Management Solutions, on February 22, 2021
7. Jeremy Hobson and Allison Hagan, "Hard Seltzer Spikes in Popularity," WBUR, September 11, 2019, www.wbur.org/hereandnow/2019/09/11/spiked-seltzers-spectacular-summer
8. Emily Heil, "The Key to White Claw's Surging Popularity: Marketing to a Post-gender World," *Washington Post*, September 10, 2019, www.washingtonpost.com/news/voraciously/wp/2019/09/10/the-key-to-white-claws-surging-popularity-marketing-to-a-post-gender-world
9. Tom Maloney, "Hard Seltzer Craze Makes White Claw Maker a Multibillionaire," Bloomberg, November 8, 2019, www.bloomberg.com/news/articles/2019-11-08/hard-seltzer-craze-makes-white-claw-creator-a-multibillionaire
10. "Profile: Anthony von Mandl," *Forbes*, May 9, 2022, www.forbes.com/profile/anthony-von-mandl/?sh=6b70bae42482
11. Doug Quackenbos, et al., "Does your company have what it takes to go global?" *Harvard Business Review*, April 2016.
12. Ibid.
13. Conversation with Sree Sivanandan, managing partner of NetworkOnomy Ventures, on February 11, 2021
14. Pierre Condamine, "The Story of Too Good To Go," Zero Waste Europe, 2020.
15. Our Story, Too Good To Go website, Accessed February 14, 2021, toogoodtogo.com/en-us
16. Alisha Coleman-Jensen, et al., "Household Food Security in the United States in 2020," U.S. Dept Agriculture, September 2021, www.ers.usda.gov/publications/pub-details/?pubid=102075
17. Pierre Condamine, "The Story of Too Good To Go," Zero Waste Europe, 2020.

18. Shoshi Parks, "Food Waste-Fighting App Too Good to Go Makes Its San Francisco Debut," 7x7 website, May 6, 2021, www.7x7.com/too-good-to-go-app-bay-area-2652891835.html
19. Conversation with Jonas Mallisse, vice president of Global Expansion for Too Good To Go, on February 12, 2021
20. Allyssia Alleyne, "These Are the Startups to Watch After the Pandemic," *Wired*, May 25, 2021, www.wired.co.uk/article/startups-after-pandemic

5

Timing Is Everything

When is the right time to enter the U.S. market? Or, if you're already doing business here: When is the right time to scale your activities? These are not easy decisions, and being too early or late can be costly and potentially damage your business operations in other countries.

In my conversations with international businesspeople, more than half said they worried about timing their U.S. market entry. They struggled with how to determine whether their organization was ready for such a move, or not. Several entrepreneurs were unsure about timing their startup launch. This chapter, therefore, focuses on timing. Although I'd initially thought of tucking this topic into the previous chapter on planning for success, it is much too important.

To help you with timing decisions, I'll share a strategic framework to identify and evaluate market conditions and external factors. I'll also cover internal factors and people considerations to consider. There are a couple of handy checklists for assessing if you are ready. And I'll offer a few ways to get a closer look at U.S. markets. The chapter ends with a case study on a German window company that timed its U.S. expansion totally wrong—yes, it missed its "window of opportunity."

Timing and the U.S. Market

If you are lucky, you might be told exactly when the right time is to enter the U.S. market. That was the case with Radical

Tea Towel. A family business, it started in Wales selling items for kitchen and home that were imprinted with political and social statements from historic literary figures, suffragettes, and freedom fighters including Che Guevara and Mahatma Gandhi.[1] Sales were direct to British consumers through a U.K. website, but news of the company and products spread over social media. Americans soon started buying tea towels, too, even though we call them "dish towels" here.

In 2016, Radical Tea Towels decided to enter the United States because of pleas they received in letters and emails, such as this one: "Please come over to the United States—our politics are such a mess; we really need the support right now, and I think there'd be great market for your designs! Think about it!" So, the company set up a U.S. website that sold dish towels featuring quotes from American radical thinkers, including Henry David Thoreau, Emma Goldman, Martin Luther King Jr., and George Orwell. The towels are still made in the United Kingdom, but they established a U.S. subsidiary and utilized a Pennsylvania fulfillment company to ship the goods.[2]

Most companies, however, don't get the benefit of U.S. consumers begging for their products. In most cases, you will need to decide whether to enter the market early into your business's life cycle or wait until you are better prepared. But consider this: If your product is one of the first of its kind to enter the U.S. market, you could secure the best resources and talent for a competitive advantage. Because you're there first, you could have access to the best store locations, suppliers, or distributors. In fact, the company that is first to enter a particular market segment can even secure the best lawyers, investment bankers, and advertising agencies. This phenomenon is known as *first-mover advantage*.

First-mover advantage can foster brand leadership and loyal customers, which makes things hard for later entrants. Brand leaders generally have higher sales volumes, lower production costs, and greater profits than competitors. First movers create new categories. The French company Danone entered the United States in 1942 and created a new category of fruity yogurt that appealed to Americans' taste for sweeter foods. Its Dannon brand continues to be the industry leader, with 33 percent of the more than $7 billion U.S. yogurt market.[3]

First-mover advantage is particularly powerful in the business-to-business (B2B) and technology industries. Businesses look for new technologies and suppliers that will give them a boost against the competition. Information technology (IT) executives will readily test and buy software, even from new startups, if it promises to speed operations or reduce cost. The online auction site eBay was the first of its kind in 1995, and it has remained the market leader, with approximately 160 million active users in 2022.[4] It even survived a well-funded Amazon Auction entry in 1999 that couldn't overcome eBay's first-mover advantage. Amazon quietly stopped supporting the service two years later.[5]

Therefore, you want to avoid being late to market, because competitors could already be established. Here's another example: A few years ago, a Canadian market startup asked my consulting firm to help with its U.S. entry. The company had developed an app that enabled marketers to conduct consumer research through its smartphone application. The startup had several customers in Canada, and the founders wanted to enter the much larger U.S. market. Unfortunately, we uncovered at least six companies already selling a similar app here. We told the entrepreneurs not to launch in the United States unless it introduced a product with much better, highly desired features.

And yet, being *second* to market sometimes has its advantages. "Early followers" can learn from the mistakes of the first-market entry. Second and third competitors benefit from the efforts of the pioneer to educate and establish a market. Tivo introduced the first video-media recorder in 1999. It spent millions of dollars on advertising to explain to skeptical consumers the benefits of DVR time-shifting to change their ingrained television watching habits. Philips Electronics, Sony, and other companies followed with less-expensive DVRs that ended up capturing a greater share of the market that Tivo developed.

In other words, despite all of the advantages of being first to place your product in a particular market, beware of entering a market *too* early. U.S. consumers might not be ready for your product or solutions. Webvan and Kozmos introduced ecommerce sites in the 1990s for groceries and household items. Both were colossal failures because the market wasn't ready for online shopping. People were hesitant to enter their credit card and personal information into a computer. It wasn't until the pandemic began that groceries purchased online became popular. Online sales grew to 8.1 percent share in 2020, and it's projected to surpass 20 percent of the U.S. grocery retail market by 2026.[6]

How do you determine if you are too early or too late to enter the U.S. market? The first step is to identify the external trends and factors that impact your industry.

What External Forces Affect Your Industry?

You can't control or easily change forces that affect your industry from the outside. These factors are the same for all competitors in any given industry. For example, every player in the energy industry is faced with growing concerns about global warming and pending government regulations. Some organizations, such as renewable energy companies, are better aligned to address climate change issues. Others, such as the big oil companies, are poorly positioned to respond to the challenge.

By using the analytic framework PESTLE taught in business schools, you can identify and categorize external factors. PESTLE is an acronym for the six major categories, which I have listed here along with several factors that might affect your industry vis-à-vis the U.S. market. Note that each category refers specifically to an aspect of the market situation that might be in flux at any given time.

POLITICAL

- Bilateral relations with your home country (e.g., talks among political leaders)

- Federal, state, and local tax policies and enforcement
- Government spending and budget trends
- Immigration policies and enforcement
- International trading policies (e.g., tariffs and trade relations)

ECONOMIC

- Availability of credit from banks and other lenders
- Disposable income trends (i.e., money that people have available to spend)
- Foreign currency exchange rates
- Inflation rates and projections
- Unemployment rates and trends

SOCIOCULTURAL

- Consumer buying patterns
- Demographic shifts (e.g., population's size, age, ethnicity, education)
- Lifestyle changes (e.g., eating and exercise behavior)
- Media consumption habits that impact advertisers' ability to reach consumers
- Societal issues (e.g., racial justice, income inequality, climate change)

TECHNOLOGY

- Adoption of new technologies (e.g., artificial intelligence, blockchain)
- Data privacy issues and policies that impact marketing and business operations
- Energy technologies (e.g., wind and solar, battery storage)
- Research discoveries that might disrupt industries and companies
- Patent protection issues that affect existing and new market entries

LEGAL

- Consumer protection laws and trends
- Employment laws and local enforcement
- Environmental laws and policies
- Intellectual property laws (e.g., patents and trademarks)
- Tax laws and local regulations

ENVIRONMENTAL

- Climate change
- Environmental activism
- Pollution issues
- Water issues
- Worker migration

Once you've considered each of the forces in the PESTLE framework, the next step is to assess how important each factor is to your industry (i.e., how much each factor might affect your ability to do business in the United States or not) and how well your organization can respond to them. The case study later in this chapter describes how Menck Fenster was impacted by sociopolitical and energy/environmental technology factors.

Because the PESTLE framework will lead to identifying dozens, if not hundreds, of external factors that might impact your industry, the strategic tool we teach in business schools is the External Factor Evaluation (EFE) Matrix. The EFE Matrix will help you to *prioritize the most important factors you've identified*—and to assess your organization's ability to respond to them.

External Factor Evaluation Matrix

To build an EFE Matrix, start by creating a table with three columns. (See the sample matrix in Figure 5.1.) In the first column, list all the external factors that might impact your effort to bring your business to the United States. Still in that first column, categorize these factors into two sections: opportunities and threats. For example, a threat would be rising unemployment that reduces the number of people who could afford your product. On the other hand, if you're selling a low-priced item, rising unemployment could be an opportunity to win new customers.

External Factor	Weight of Importance	Ability to Respond	Weighted Score
Opportunities:			
1. Proliferation of computers in business	.1	4	.4
2. Increased attention on cybersecurity	.3	5	1.5
3. Stakeholders demand reduced risk	.2	4	.8
Threats:			
4. More companies outsource IT function	.2	3	.6
5. Uncertain economy delays IT purchases	.2	2	.4
Totals	1.0	-----	3.7

Company's ability to respond: 5 = superior, 4 = above average, 3 = average, 2 = below average, 1 = poor

Figure 5.1 EFE Matrix Example

In the next column, assign to each factor a weight of importance from 0.0 (not important) to 1.0 (very important). The sum of all the weights should equal 1.0. For example, data security is important in the banking industry, so the impact of rising cyberattacks would be high, and you'd give it a high weight.

In the last column, assign a rating from 1 to 5 on how well your organization is able to effectively respond to each factor you've listed (5 = superior response; 4 = above average; 3 = average with industry competitors; 2 = below average response; 1 = poor ability to respond). Therefore, if your software product utilizes the most advanced cybersecurity technology, you'd assign a high score of 5 or 4 to that factor.

What Internal Factors Might Affect Your Timing?

Apart from the external forces just described, you'll also find that various factors within your organization will affect the decisions you make around when to enter the United States. Your organization must have the necessary people, products, resources, and processes in place to be successful in a competitive market. Even if there is a huge opportunity in the U.S. market, it still may be too early for your particular organization if it isn't yet capable and ready.

Thoroughly examining the internal factors, then, starts with taking an audit of the strengths and weaknesses in the key functional areas, including sales, marketing, finance, human resources, and legal. Ideally, you would interview people in both senior and junior roles to glean a true picture of the organization's capabilities. Does the current team have experience and knowledge of business in U.S. markets? Look for any deficiencies or weaknesses that you might be able to fix or offset by hiring or adding external people and organizations.

Next, examine your manufacturing capacities, supply chain operations, and information systems. Will you be able to scale to meet the demands of U.S. markets? If you're an entrepreneur, is your startup at the right stage of development? If not, a viable strategy might be to enter a region or a smaller U.S. market. This could be the beachhead for further expansion later as capabilities grow. Another option could be a joint venture with another company to fill production or supply chain gaps.

In addition, evaluate the products you plan to introduce to U.S. customers and consumers. Your product will need to be both distinctly different and offer more value than competitors in ways that are important to buyers. Your products might need to be tailored for the United States, particularly the packaging language and legal requirements. Don't assume that success in your home country will spell success here. You may need to test your product's value proposition in the United States either in a market-research study or in a test market that represents a limited risk for your company.

"It's easy to go too fast or be too early with the U.S. launch before the company is prepared to take this challenge. It's a differently structured and hyper-competitive market," lamented Rytis Vitkauskas, co-founder and CEO of YPlan.[7] Rytis struggled to enter U.S. markets in 2014 only to sell the U.K. company for approximately $1 million in stock two years later. Not a great result, considering that investors had pumped more than $30 million into the venture.[8]

Pioneers Needed

It's important to honestly assess the pioneering individuals you plan to place on your U.S. initiative team. If you intend to send executives to the United States, they will need a diverse set of skills navigating the different cultures and ways of doing business. The expats will need to be talented managers and market development people with a high level of commitment and energy. They can't be easily discouraged or inclined to avoid risk. As Bruce Buchanan, CEO of Rokt told me, your expat managers will need resilience, toughness, and grit. Why? "Because when your building something from the ground up or you're trying to migrate a business from another country to the United States," he said, "a lot of things are going to be bloody tough."[9]

These pioneers need to be brave, too. They need to fully commit to the mission without worrying about their future. If the mission doesn't meet senior management's expectations, will those pioneers be able to return to their home country and resume their careers? Virtually every international company executive that attempted to enter the United States told me that they underestimated the length of time and cost of establishing a foothold here. One executive at a Global 250 recounted how he returned home after a three-year commitment in another country to find no job and no office waiting for him.

If the expat has a family, will their spouses and children need support and guidance? Schools are very different in the United States, so it could be challenging for families on many dimensions. Luckily, many cities have schools for international children that teach in multiple languages. Some offer International Baccalaureate (IB) degrees so that students can continue their studies in their home countries. This is particularly valuable for colleges and universities in home countries that offer lower tuition costs for their citizens.

U.S. Readiness Checklist

When you've considered all of the issues I've just outlined and the timing looks promising, then you're ready to arrange for your entry and/or expansion into the U.S. market. There's a lot to think about, particularly because of the complexity and number of unknowns. A good way to prepare is with a checklist. If checklists can help airplane pilots prepare for a flight, they can help you get ready for your journey.

Professor and surgeon Dr. Atul Gawande wrote how checklists can dramatically improve performance in complex situations requiring quick decisions.[10] Proven in medical emergency rooms and airplane cockpits, checklists can help everyone prepare for complex procedures. Certainly, entering and expanding in the United States is complex and requires fast decision-making that would benefit from a checklist.

To assist in developing Go-to-U.S. market checklists, I sought the advice of Soft Land Partners (SLP), a consortium of professionals that helps international companies enter new markets. SLP Founder Bill Kenney is also a sailor, and he knows the value of ocean charts that reveal rocks, hazards, and adverse currents. Bill views business checklists as a tool to chart potential obstacles and pitfalls in a new market. That way, he says, foreign businesspeople "can navigate to the best partners and resources easily."

Working with the SLP task force, I gathered dozens of checklists and readiness assessment tools published by academics, consultants, and investor firms. We then organized and edited them into a checklist of questions that companies should answer before attempting U.S. expansions. Afterward, I confirmed the checklist's efficacy by vetting it with business, law, and finance professionals. I also vetted the checklist we created for startups with entrepreneurs and new venture investors. (See both checklists in the appendixes.)

All of those people agreed, moreover, that no foreign company should attempt to break into the U.S. market without first doing its homework—including spending some time addressing everything on the checklist. That advice is especially true for startups. As Ian Houston, the president of the Scottish Business Network, advised, "When I think of entrepreneurship, not lost on me is the 'ship.' We need a vessel to take us where we want to go. One must put the hard work into building it, then we map out the journey and hoist the sail."[11]

First Steps

When it comes to determining the right time to enter the U.S. market—or whether you should attempt it at all—it's particularly difficult if you are physically located in another country. Nevertheless, you can take some exploratory first steps. Besides using checklists and considering external and internal factors, you might consider working with an outside agency that could help you learn more about U.S. market factors and opportunity. Such a move would also enable you to start building a network of advisors, connections, and sales prospects.

Luckily, there are many organizations and resources available to help you investigate U.S. markets and trends. For entrepreneurs, there are 2,165 startup accelerators and incubators across the country.[12] Many have programs specifically designed for international startups and scale-ups.

Here is an overview of the types of programs to consider for your first stage of entry and expansion:

- **Immersion and tourism programs.** These are government trade and economic development organizations that offer short programs to learn about U.S. business. For example, the U.S. Department of Commerce's Select USA runs two-week programs to tour a region for international businesspeople. BelCham of Belgium and other chambers of commerce offer intensive programs—typically one-week—in U.S. cities to meet industry experts, investors, mentors, and expats. Other private organizations offer "tourism" programs to see the offices and meet with U.S. businesses and advisors.

- **Educational institutions.** American colleges and universities offer foreign students many options for learning about U.S. business. Some are geared for intensive immersion and study. Many offer noncredit courses without having to enroll in a degree or certificate program. Industry associations and private organizations have stepped into the education arena, too. The French-American Chamber of Commerce partnered with NYU, Columbia, Insead, and HEC Paris on an executive certificate program for international business.
- **Accelerators.** Typically, accelerator programs are for six months with access to office space, education, networking events, industry experts, and mentors. Accelerators are usually run by investment funds or private organizations and focus on industries ranging from agriculture to education and financial technologies. Several accelerators, including WEVE Acceleration, focus on helping international companies and entrepreneurs grow in the United States in a "soft landing" without taking an equity share. Canadian Technology Accelerators (CTA) has programs in Boston, New York City, San Francisco, and Silicon Valley that help Canadian companies with U.S. expansion.
- **Incubators.** Incubator programs offer entrepreneurs office space and access to advisors, lawyers, investors, and other resources. Unlike accelerators, there are no time limits in incubators. Incubators typically provide investments of $25,000 to $50,000 in exchange for 5 percent to 6 percent of the company's equity.[13] TechStars and Y Combinator are two prestigious ones; they accept only a small number of startups that apply to their programs. The New York City Economic Development Corporation launched In2NYC to help foreign-born entrepreneurs qualify for a Cap-Exempt H-1B visa (visas above the

governments' 85,000 limit). Recently, large firms, including Google and Chobani, have created incubator programs for entrepreneurial ventures.

- **Trade shows**. Virtually every industry—from antiques and cybersecurity to specialty foods—has trade shows, which are an excellent way to see the products, competitors, and marketing activities. You can even hire someone knowledgeable about that industry as a guide. David Polinchock, a veteran of AT&T technology research, runs Experience WalkAbouts at the Consumer Electronics Show (CES) and other technology industry events. With 4,500 exhibitors across 2.9 million square feet, CES can be frustrating to navigate for a newcomer. David gives people the "lay of the land" on the context, business practices, and trends in each industry segment.

Well, it's "about time" to wrap up this topic of timing your entry into the United States. In our next chapter, you'll learn how to determine where in the U.S. market to target your business. Before moving on, however, be sure to see the case study about an international company that failed because it misjudged the timing of its U.S. expansion.

Case Study: Menck Fenster (Germany)

Menck Fenster GmbH is a 130-year-old window manufacturer based in Hamburg, Germany. After many years of selling high-quality, wooden-framed windows in North America through local distributors, it decided to expand its U.S. operation. To help fund the effort, it created a joint venture with Liesenfeld International, a Hamburg-based

(*continued*)

(*continued*)

logistics company. The two companies believed they could dramatically increase revenue by providing more options, faster delivery, and better service to architects and builders in North America.

Menck's windows and doors are among the most advanced in the world. Its excellence in engineering and precise manufacturing produced wood-framed windows to the most exacting measurements. Along with other German companies, Menck's products surpassed all others for energy efficiency and Leadership in Energy and Environmental Design (LEED) compliance.

Given the company's global leadership, its management felt the time was right for U.S. expansion. "Window and door innovation is at least 10 years more advanced in Europe than in the United States," said Todd F. Bachelder, president of Menck USA. "It's important for industry professionals to see for themselves the innovative technology, creativity, and ingenuity that goes into every Menck window and door, each of which is manufactured using the same advanced energy-efficiency requirements and manufacturing processes used in Europe."[14]

In 2015, Menck opened a modern factory in Chicopee, Massachusetts, for its Menck USA joint venture. It featured advanced, computer-controlled woodworking equipment that was new to the U.S. market. The joint venture received $750,000 in investment tax credits from the state government in Massachusetts. The city of Chicopee gave the company a special tax assessment valued at around $350,000. And MassDevelopment, the state's finance and development agency, issued a $5 million tax-exempt bond on behalf of Menck USA to fund the project. In return, Menck USA promised to hire 50 people over a five-year period in the factory.[15]

Within two years, Menck closed its factory and put it up for sale. An executive from Boston Private Bank, which had purchased $5 million of bonds, explained that investors, who had already made $14 million in capital contributions and loans, lost faith in the venture. Production costs were more expensive than Menck anticipated. The factory took longer to build than predicted, and it was difficult training employees hired in Chicopee because its equipment was so complex. Sales started slowly overall and weren't growing fast enough.[16]

What Went Wrong?

While the market for windows in the United States is huge, Menck focused on a relatively small segment for premium products. Wood windows are primarily used in family homes and restorations of older buildings designed by architects. Windows for office and apartment buildings represent the bulk of industry sales. Builders generally use aluminum or vinyl windows, which require less maintenance and cost less.

Menck competed in the premium segment because its windows were significantly more expensive than the market-leading American companies: Andersen, Marvin, and Pella. Also, Merck specialized in European-style windows with a handle that twists up and enables someone to pull the window into the room rather than pushing it out. U.S. homeowners prefer casement windows that turn out or double-hung windows that slide up and down.

Bad timing was another cause of Menck's failure. When the new factory opened, the market for new homes and buildings was still depressed from the 2008–2010 credit crash. Imported industrial supplies and materials was 45 percent lower in 2016 than its peak in 2008.

(*continued*)

(*continued*)

At that time, energy prices were much lower in the United States than Europe. Homeowners were reluctant to replace old windows with more energy-efficient ones, because they wouldn't repay their investment for decades. Eventually, there will be more regulations and cultural pressure for LEED-compliant buildings and use of energy-efficient building materials, such as what Menck supplies. But until then, the decision to use these advanced windows is more emotional (for people who wish to be ecologically conscious) than financial.

Joey Karas, president of Karas and Karas Glass in Boston, said that Menck chose the wrong place to build a high-tech factory. Joey is an industry expert who has worked for more than 40 years at the glass company his grandfather founded. Their family-owned business has survived when many others have failed in the competitive industry. Smartly, they chose to only supply glass to window companies to avoid the high cost of labor and machinery required to manufacture framed windows.

Joey questioned whether Menck was able to find the right skill base of the employees in western Massachusetts. The sophisticated computer-enabled equipment often requires months of training by engineers or craftspeople. He saw other companies purchase million-dollar pieces of specialty equipment only to find them underutilized because they didn't have the trained, skilled people able to run them.

He thought the decision to bring sales in-house rather than use distributors was problematic. Each region had different building needs and regulations. In Miami there were regulations and specifications about wind resistance for hurricanes. In California, there were regulations about earthquake resistance. Some areas had stricter requirements about energy efficiency. It made it more challenging and costly when responding to buyer and contractors' questions. That made bringing the sales in-house more challenging.

Lessons from This Case Study:

1. **Be realistic about market size.** While the overall U.S. window market is huge, Menck competed in the high-end segment of expensive new homes and renovations. Therefore, the total addressable market (TAM) was significantly smaller.
2. **Choose the right time.** The TAM had still not recovered from the 2008–2010 depression. Also, the market for energy-efficient windows had not developed to support Menck's expansion effort. It would have been better to have kept their relationship with the American distributor and wait to expand.
3. **Learn what the U.S. market wants.** Don't assume that success in your home country will translate to U.S. markets. Menck failed because it arrogantly thought Americans would want its superior product.
4. **Consider the talent you will need when selecting a location.** Menck did not consider the number of skilled workers needed to run its high-tech factory and miscalculated the amount of time needed to get them trained on their operation. They also underestimated the industry experience needed to complete complex sales.

Notes

1. "Our Story," Radical Tea Towel, Accessed September 9, 2021, www.radicalteatowel.com/our-story
2. Alison Coleman, "Meet The Brits Who've Expanded Their Businesses To The U.S.," *Forbes*, July 30, 2019, www.forbes.com/sites/alisoncoleman/2019/07/30/meet-the-brits-whove-expanded-their-businesses-to-the-us

3. Christopher Doering, "Danone US Yogurt Chief "Bullish" Despite Segment's Broader Struggles," Food Dive, January 15, 2020, www.fooddive.com/news/danone-us-yogurt-chief-bullish-despite-segments-broader-struggles/569708
4. "EBay Revenue and Usage Statistics (2022)" Business of Apps. December 15, 2021, www.businessofapps.com/data/ebay-statistics
5. "Amazon Auction," Failory, Accessed April 16, 2022, www.failory.com/amazon/auction
6. Russell Redman, "E-Commerce to account for 20% of U.S. grocery market by 2026," Supermarket News, October 22, 2021, www.supermarketnews.com/online-retail/e-commerce-account-20-us-grocery-market-2026
7. Octopus Ventures, "Question the Questions: Applying some Socrates to your U.S. expansion plans," 2018.
8. Sam Shead, "Time Out has bought London events startup YPlan for £1.6 million," Business Insider, Accessed August 25, 2021, www.businessinsider.com/time-out-acquires-yplan-2016-10
9. Conversation with Bruce Buchanan, CEO and founder of Rokt, on March 23, 2021
10. Atul Gawande. "A Life-Saving Checklist," *The New Yorker*, December 3, 2007, www.newyorker.com/magazine/2007/12/10/the-checklist
11. Conversation with Ian Houston, president of the Scottish Business Network, on February 22, 2022
12. Tracxn, "Accelerators & Incubators in United States," March 30, 2022, tracxn.com/d/investor-lists/Accelerators-&-Incubators-in-United-States
13. David S. Rose, *Angel Investing* (Hoboken, NJ: John Wiley & Sons, Inc., 2014), p.164
14. Area Development, "Germany-based Menck Windows Establishes Manufacturing Facility in Chicopee, Massachusetts," May 5, 2015, www.areadevelopment.com/newsitems/5-5-2015/menck-windows-manufacturing-facility-chicopee-massachusetts189434.shtml
15. Jim Kinney, "Menck USA: What happens to tax breaks, loan guarantee?" MassLive, January 24, 2017, www.masslive.com/business-news/2017/01/menck_usa_window_factory_has_shut_down_w.html
16. Ibid.

6

Where to Play

Just as an actor needs a stage and a baseball player needs a diamond-shaped field, you need a clearly defined place to grow your business, a "place to play." There are many decisions to factor in when deciding where to land your business in the United States. In addition to which marketplaces to compete and where to locate your offices, where-to-play decisions include product category, channel of sales, distribution method, and stage in the value chain.

Consider a South American salt company that aims to do business in the United States. Which markets of consumers should it target? Should it open a U.S. office? If so, in what city? To sell what types of products—bath salts, cooking salts, or table salts? Will it ship the salts to the United States in individual packages or in bulk containers? If packaged in the United States, will it be produced in company-owned buildings or subcontracted to a local factory? And how will it be sold? Directly online to customers, in supermarkets, or through a distributor to smaller stores?

The places you select can dramatically affect your venture's success. International companies often try to enter the U.S. market without clearly defining its parameters and determining how to reach customers effectively. As Federico Tozzi, executive director of the Italy-American Chamber of Commerce, told me, too many European businesspeople say they will "discover" their plan once they get here.[1]

Choosing where *not to* play is important, too. It may seem counterintuitive, but your company or brand will have greater success within a narrowly defined playing field than in a broad, loosely defined marketplace.[2] That way, you will compete against fewer competitors, and you'll better understand the needs and wants of your customers. If you're with a smaller company, you can better handle capacity and scalability in a smaller playing field. And you can have closer relationships with local distribution and channel partners.

This chapter focuses on where-to-play decisions that are core to your Go-to-U.S. strategy. Noteworthy, these decisions are closely linked to your timing, product selection, and marketing decisions discussed in other chapters. It could be too early to enter one market segment but the perfect time to enter another. You can arrive late to the game and still become the market leader if you introduce a value-packed product delivered in a more convenient and attractive way. This chapter ends with a case study of a Belgian company, Renson, that made many where-to-play decisions when it entered the United States. Before we dive into the topic of where-to-play decisions, let's first address a common misperception about America.

The United States Is Not One Homogenous Country

Many people living outside the United States think it is one homogeneous country. The founder of an Australian company told me they plan to enter the United States because it is one huge market that speaks one language and has one set of rules. Compared with Europe's 44 countries, that assumption is correct: The United States is easier to navigate. However, it is a mistake to underestimate the complexity and diversity in our country.

Anyone who has traveled within the United States knows that each region is unique. And within each region, there are huge differences between states, counties, cities, and neighborhoods. In each community, people have varying beliefs, behaviors, and lifestyles. Even the pace and use of language shift depending on the location. Californians think, talk, and behave very differently than Texans, who are very different than Virginians and Wisconsinites. And New Yorkers, well, "Fuhgeddaboudit"! They are so unlike anyone else in the country.

The land and climates of the United States also fluctuate greatly across its more than 3.8 million square miles (6 million square meters) of land. In fact, the U.S. Department of Commerce's Oceanic and Atmospheric Administration recognizes five different climate zones, ranging from tropical to dry, and the physical landscapes within these U.S. regions vary from flat plains to tall mountains, lush forests to barren dirt fields. Water and other natural resources range in availability from abundant to skimpy depending on the location.

Each of our 50 states has its own set of laws and regulations. Taxes vary from state to state, county to county, and city to city. California's state sales tax is 7.25%, but with sales taxes added in each county and city, residents pay more than 10% taxes on goods purchased.[3] New Hampshire and four other states have no state or local sales taxes. Moreover, regulations on employment practices and other business activities differ by state, county, and municipality.

Why So Much Difference Across Regions?

From the beginning, the United States has never been truly united. It was cobbled together in 1776 from 13 colonies that were practically separate nations. Each North American colony was founded by immigrants from distinct regions of the British Isles, France, the Netherlands, and Spain—each with its own religious, political and ethnographic traits. They saw themselves as competitors for land, capital, and new settlers; some colonists viewed the others as enemies.[4]

The original colonies united to form one nation only to revolt when the British monarchy levied exorbitant taxes, restricted trade with France and Spain, and tried to stop land speculators—including George Washington, Benjamin Franklin, and Thomas Jefferson—from claiming new territories from Native Americans.[5]

American Nations, by Colin Woodard, tells the history of the 11 rival regional cultures of North America.[6] Each culture was formed by a distinct group of mostly European immigrants, each with its own beliefs, values, behaviors, and dialects. Woodard describes how these groups stayed mostly apart from each other for several generations. Then, over the past 100 years, they migrated and integrated into other regions. Nonetheless, these regional differences still exist in the United States, and Woodard assigns each region a name that reflects its origins (see Figure 6.1).

> **Yankeedom** was founded on the shores of Massachusetts Bay by the Puritans and Pilgrims who left England searching for religious freedom. From the New England states,

Figure 6.1 Map of American nations today
Source: Tufts Magazine/Colin Woodard

the Yankee culture—so named by British soldiers as an insult to the early settlers—spread across the upper Midwest and New York. While religious zeal has waned in Yankee nation, there is still strong belief in education, intellectual achievement, communal empowerment, and broad citizen participation in politics and government.

New Netherland stems from Dutch traders who sailed to the Hudson River in the early 1600s. At the time, the Netherlands was the most sophisticated and tolerant society in the Western world. From the beginning, New Netherland had a global commercial culture, which has been described as "materialistic, with a tolerance for ethnic and religious diversity and an unflinching commitment to the freedom of inquiry and conscience."[7] Over the years, the spirit of commerce, freedom, and diversity has only grown stronger in this region surrounding New York City.

The Midlands was founded by the English Quakers, who believed in peoples' inherent goodness and welcomed people from many ethnic and religious backgrounds. They first settled along the Delaware Bay, including sections of New Jersey, Pennsylvania, Delaware and Maryland. This cultural nation later expanded across the middle of the country. Immigrants to the Midlands brought with them a strong belief in equality, honest dialogue, and a collective community. The culture, which still exists today, has been described as pluralistic and organized around the middle class.[8]

The Tidewater region was created by younger sons of English gentry who settled on the rich and fertile soil surrounding Chesapeake Bay in the early 1600s. It then expanded to parts of Virginia, Maryland, Delaware, and North Carolina. The early settlers tried to reproduce the semi-feudal society of their home country, which included indentured servants and, later, slaves. Tidewater's conservative culture placed high value on authority and tradition, with little value on equality or public participation in politics. Once powerful, this cultural nation has been in decline with encroachment from Greater Appalachia and erosion within Washington, D.C., and Norfolk.[9]

Greater Appalachia describes the region in the highlands west of Tidewater. Waves of settlers came in the early 18th century from Ireland, northern England, and Scotland to escape wars and famines. They brought a culture that has been characterized by a warrior ethic and a commitment to personal sovereignty and individual liberty. Even today the people of Greater Appalachia are known to be proud, independent, and somewhat volatile. This cultural region has expanded westward into parts of Ohio, Indiana, Illinois, Arkansas, and Oklahoma.[10]

The Deep South nation was founded in the 1670s by English slave lords from Barbados who landed in South Carolina looking to grow cotton, rice, and other crops. They proceeded to create a West Indies–style slave society based on cruelty and violence, where democracy was the privilege of just a few citizens.[11] White supremacy and concentrated wealth proliferated in those days and continued even beyond the Civil War and the end of slavery, until well into the 20th century. This regional culture expanded to Georgia, Mississippi, Florida, and parts of Texas. The Deep South has changed for the better with each new generation, but its brutal beginning cannot be forgotten. Nonetheless, people in this cultural region are still known to fight against federal regulations and taxes on its wealthy.

New France was established in the early 1600s by French fur traders around Québec. Settlers sought to escape the feudal political and social restrictions established with the Kingdom of France. Their good relations with native tribes in North America led to a multicultural, egalitarian, and consensus-driven culture. A group from New France migrated to New Orleans to create an American outpost. Proud of their French heritage and independence, it has remained one of the most liberal of all regional cultures where diversity and negotiated consensus are valued.

The Far West lies just inward from the Pacific coast in areas of California, Oregon, Washington, Idaho, and Montana. It is defined more by its environment of dry and rocky land and high elevations than ethnographic factors. This "second-generation" regional nation was founded by people who migrated from elsewhere to work in its mines, railroads, factories, and cattle ranches. Settlements were determined by mining and industrial companies or the federal government that controlled most of the land. Cultural beliefs in the Far West remain focused on hard work, family values, and independence. Today Far Westerners focus their anger on the federal government rather than the corporations who brought them there.[12]

The Left Coast region spans the Pacific Ocean from Monterey, California, to Juneau, Alaska. It includes the four progressive cities of San Francisco, Portland, Seattle, and Vancouver. The cultural nation was founded by New England woodworkers, missionaries, and merchants along with Greater Appalachian farmers and prospectors. Left Coast culture is a blend of Yankeedom's idealism and intellectualism with Greater Appalachia's values of self-expression, independence, and exploration.[13] Often its people clash with Far Westerners who also live in these U.S. states.

El Norte was actually the first regional culture, because it was formed by Spanish soldiers and missionaries in the late 1500s. They built communities in the region now marked by the U.S.-Mexico border along Texas, Arizona, and New Mexico. El Norte is known for its

Hispanic language, culture, and rituals. In Mexico, "Norteños" have the reputation for being independent, hardworking, adaptable, and self-sufficient. El Norte has always seen itself as a distinctly different nation than the rest of the country.

Where Will You "Set Up Shop"?

Since every U.S. region is, and always has been, very culturally and physically different, the area that you as a businessperson choose to enter has huge implications. Within each region, there are smaller markets of states, counties, cities, towns, and neighborhoods. Even if you plan to expand across all 50 states, you'll still need to prioritize which markets to enter first and which don't warrant a marketing investment. Think of the market you enter as the playing field or chessboard where you begin your U.S. initiative.

Initially, it will be important to establish a U.S. headquarters rather than try to do business from your home country. Customers, suppliers, and distributors prefer to do business with local rather than foreign companies. They generally don't care if it is subsidiary, as long as the business in conducted along American rules and regulations. Their legal teams want business contracts written under U.S. laws, and they don't want to venture outside the country if there are legal disputes.

Many international software as a service (SaaS) and technology-driven companies are able to sell to the United States remotely. However, at some point they find they need to establish a steady U.S. presence. ProxyClick was able to sell its visitor-management applications to U.S. enterprises remotely from Belgium. However, it was too difficult to support U.S. clients, such as Airbnb, from its headquarters in the Central European Time (CET) zone. ProxyClick's first U.S.-based employee, therefore, was someone hired to ensure "customer success."

Tobias Reisner from Karlsruhe, Germany, is a co-founder and Global Partner of Human Design Technology International, which designs and produces clothing for people with disabilities. With operations in Moscow and collaborations with British design schools, the company gained attention at fashion shows in Russia and Europe. After a positive debut at the L.A. Fashion Show in 2016, Tobias decided to set up manufacturing facilities in California under a U.S. business entity. He'd realized it would be difficult to manage and communicate with American workers remotely, even with videoconferencing. He had seen other companies try to enter the U.S. market from afar—only to lose money because of wasted time because of misunderstandings.[14]

For companies that market tangible products, you'll need distribution and warehousing locations as you scale. At some point, it may be cheaper and faster to produce your products in a U.S. factory. MAS Holdings is a $2 billion textile company headquartered in Sri Lanka. For more than 30 years, it has designed, developed, and produced sportswear, intimate apparel, and swimwear for major brands, including Nike, Lululemon, and Victoria's Secret.[15] It has manufacturing facilities across 17 countries including the United States. In 2017, MAS Holdings bought a manufacturing facility in North Carolina to provide "the most flexible speed to market solutions to our customers from design, prototyping, manufacturing, and delivery to the ultimate customer."[16]

For startup and scale-up companies, a good entry point will enable your business to move faster and generate stronger results. According to VC Joe White, investors assess whether the location can help or hinder the competitiveness of companies.[17] Managed properly, a successful start will generate positive cash flow to fund further U.S. expansion. Investors, partners, and employees are more likely to jump on a ship that's sailing fast, and they'll be delighted to have an international captain at the helm.

How Will You Choose a Location?

With so many options, how do you decide which U.S. location to enter? Many factors need to be evaluated, including what fits your budget, and undoubtedly you'll be forced to make trade-offs and sacrifice one variable for another. Nonetheless, here are several key factors to consider: the potential for earning revenue; the quality and costs of the local workforce; infrastructure costs and availability; availability of capital; feeding the supply chain; regulatory and tax considerations; and economic development incentives. Let's look at each of these in turn.

Revenue Potential. Begin by identifying markets where you can grow a profitable business. For consumer product and service companies, the best strategy is to target locations with established demand. If people are already buying the category, they could be more easily persuaded to try your product. These aren't necessarily the biggest markets, but ones with the greatest concentration of existing sales and consistent customers. For example, a South American sunscreen company would target Miami rather than Chicago, even though both have 2.7 million residents. (For more on local market revenue potential, see the case study about Renson of Belgium later in the chapter.)

There are ample sources of consumer data and market research studies to identify high revenue potential markets, such as industry associations and trade publications. Mintel, IBISWorld, and Gartner offer market and industry research reports. For B2B companies, the U.S. Census Bureau provides data on U.S. businesses, including the number of establishments and employees, by state and Metropolitan Statistical Areas (MSA). Plus, there are many U.S.-based consultants and research firms that provide local market intelligence and custom research studies.

Workforce Quality and Costs. Salary costs are generally higher in the United States, particularly when including healthcare, insurance, and other benefits. Talented workers are critical to business success, especially in competitive U.S. markets. Salary cost and availability of talent vary tremendously by city and state. Look for locations with a pool of qualified workers that you could hire within your budget. The SelectUSA Stats website provides data on pay ranges by industry category and occupation for each state.[18]

If skills need to be taught, then you need to build the cost of training into your strategic plan. For example, after building a state-of-the-art factory in the Berkshire mountains of Massachusetts, the German window company Menck Fenster found there weren't nearly enough workers in that area who had the skills and experience needed to complete complicated glass-cutting and window assembly. (See the case study on Menck Fenster in Chapter 5.)

Infrastructure Costs and Availability. Choose markets with attractive and affordable office space. Flexibility and scalability are important considerations, too. Costs, which are driven by supply and demand, vary tremendously by region, city, and neighborhood. The nicest office spaces in Silicon Valley and Manhattan rent for more than $100 per square foot per year.[19] Electricity and other utility costs also should be part of the evaluation.

One option to minimize overhead costs and avoid long-term leases is to rent shared office spaces. Two of the largest workspace-sharing companies, Regus and WeWork, have facilities across the country. In addition, there are many accelerators and incubators that offer temporary offices for international companies, which they refer to as "soft landing" services. Any of these options will help you cut costs and redirect your funds to higher-priority concerns.

Availability of Capital. The location you choose can heavily influence how difficult it will be to raise investment capital. VC firms and investment funds tend to be concentrated in select cities. One VC partner in a Silicon

Valley firm famously said, "I'll never invest in a startup if I can't drive to it in one day." His views may be extreme, but there is definitely a tendency to invest in nearby business entities. If you are borrowing money, you'll find ample banking institutions in most regions of the country.

Feeding the Supply Chain. When starting your business, remember that you will not only be entering a particular market, but you'll also be entering an ecosystem. Will you have the necessary suppliers and vendors to support your growth in that region or market? Transportation costs, availability, and timing for products and materials might also play a role, particularly if you are mass-producing products. A strong ecosystem will enable companies to move faster, operate more efficiently, and deliver products and services valued by customers.

Regulatory and Tax Considerations. Each state and municipality has different regulations and tax structures. For example, every state, and many cities, had different restrictions and protocols for businesses during the COVID pandemic. Therefore, it is important to investigate them in the selection process. Tax Foundation is an independent nonprofit organization that publishes an annual report on the tax policies and climate for each state. Another nonprofit organization, The Council of State Taxation, publishes reports on tax policies and a helpful glossary of terms.

Economic Development Incentives. While incentives, such as tax rebates and lower utility costs, shouldn't drive your decision of "where to play," they should be considered. Many states and cities have an Economic Development Organization (EDO) to entice companies to locate there. They particularly want international firms that will employ local workers. Incentives might include cash grants to subsidize training, recruiting, and infrastructure costs. Other incentives include tax credits and tax exemptions for property and sales tax. In addition, incentives can help facilitate financing and leases. The U.S. Economic Development Administration website has a directory to all EDOs that offer incentives for bringing your business to their area. (You can find it at www.eda.gov.)

Where Is Your Industry Located?

International businesses entering the United States will usually first look at where their competitors are located. Companies within industries are often clustered in particular U.S. areas. Often it is where the first or biggest company in a market settled. In technical industries, companies grew around strong universities and research communities. Many Silicon Valley firms were born at nearby Stanford University and University of California, Berkeley. Engineering and skilled workers gravitate to these locations, and industry suppliers and support services are found in these ecosystems.

The U.S. Department of Commerce's Economic Development Administration partnered with Harvard Business School's Institute for Strategy and Competitiveness to study these clusters. They found that "clusters capture important linkages and potential spillovers of technology, skills, and information that cuts across firms and industries."[20] The cluster-mapping initiative collected more than 50 million open-data records on industry clusters and regional businesses. (You can find the "Map of U.S. Industry Clusters" on the OECD website.[21])

Although there are many benefits to locating your business in an industry cluster, you also might consider doing business in markets where the competition isn't present. You could provide better service or just be their best choice. For example, rather than opening a fancy French restaurant in a town that already has a couple of fine ones, it would be better to go to a town where people can't find a good coq au vin or boeuf bourguignon.

What About Lifestyle and Family Considerations?

In addition to finding a good location for your business, you need to consider life outside of work. You'll want to find a place where you and your family (if you have one) can live comfortably and find personal fulfillment. An attractive location can make it easier to entice employees in your home country to move to the United States. This section discusses some things to consider.

The Social Life. Will you (and any partners) find friends and local attractions that you'll enjoy together? Are there any expats from your country that could help with the transition? Suzanne Southard is the president of Swedish Women Educational Association International (SWEA International), which has 30 local chapters in the United States connecting and supporting Swedish expats. "It's nice to have those Swedish friends who can understand you in this very different, big country far, far away from home," Suzanne told me.[22]

Cost of Living. Housing, food, healthcare, and utility costs vary greatly among different U.S. cities. The monthly cost to rent a one-bedroom apartment is a whopping $3,100 in New York City and $2,800 in San Francisco, whereas in Chicago or Austin, Texas, you'll pay $1,500 for the same amount of space.[23] Crime rates and neighborhood safety, as well as availability of suitable transportation, are important considerations, too.

Education. If you or your colleagues have school-age children, are there suitable schools in the area? Will they provide a good education and a positive, healthy environment for them? If you are planning on staying in the United States for just a few years, are there schools that are recognized by the education system in your home country? Some locations have special high schools geared for expats with dual degrees, so they can go back to college in their home country.

Language Subleties

Sophia "Puff" Story, president of 3 Sided Cube, moved with her family to Chicago from London in early 2021. Early on, she says, her seven-year-old daughter faced some embarrassment at school: She asked to borrow a "rubber"—not knowing that Americans use the word "eraser" for the implement to remove pencil marks.

Other Where-to-Play Decisions

For larger companies with multiple product lines, a key where-to-play decision is what product and service types you want to bring the United States market. It is often unfeasible logistically and too expensive to bring entire product lines to U.S. markets. The decision should be based on which product or service offers the best opportunity in the United States, regardless of which is the strongest seller in the home country.

Andros SNC, based in France, manufactures and sells a wide variety of dairy, bakery, and other food products all around the world. But it chose to enter the U.S. market with only its Bonne Maman Preserves brand, since there was limited competition in the premium segment of the market for jams, jellies, and preserves. The big U.S. brands, Smucker's and Welch's, were focused on the traditional flavors of strawberry and grape jellies and jams. Andros saw the opportunity, therefore, for a high-quality brand made with simple ingredients offering a wider flavor selection of preserves with large pieces of fruit. Today, Bonne Maman is the number-two preserve brand in the United States.[24]

In addition, as part of your where-to-play considerations, you'll need to decide in which channels you will sell and distribute your products. Brands could reach customers through dealers, sales agents, or distributors. Selling direct to consumers (DTC) through the Internet is an increasingly viable channel, particularly for international companies that aren't ready to invest in U.S. operations.

Consider, for example, the fact that the United States has more than 38,000 grocery stores and supermarkets.[25] With that kind of volume dispersed across the country, only the largest distributors can afford to sell to and service those stores. That's how World Finer Foods (WFF) found its niche. In the 1940s, the sales and marketing company pioneered the creation of a new category of products, which became known as "specialty foods." WFF now handles marketing, sales, and logistics to distributors and retailers for more than 800 international and domestic specialty food, beverage, and personal care items. In this way, WFF enables even small brands to get a foothold in the U.S. market.

Finally, the vertical stage of production is another aspect of where-to-play decisions. There are a lot of steps and activities within the value chain—the vertical integration from product design and ingredient sourcing to production and warehousing, shipping, marketing, and eventually delivering the goods to consumers. Very few companies are involved at every single stage of the value chain. Danone manufactures and promotes its yogurts, but it lets farmers milk the cows and allows supermarkets to sell directly to consumers. Even Toyota hires design professionals in California and outsources the manufacturing of parts.

As you've seen in this chapter, there are many decisions about where to play, including the geographic market, groups of customers, products to introduce, and stage of the vertical chain. The good news is that you can test multiple options and then go with—or, as card players say, "double down" on—the ones with the most promise.

Now that you have the tools for creating an effective Go-to-U.S. market strategy, it's time to move onto implementing these plans. In the next chapter, you'll learn about the U.S. legal system and its implications for doing business here.

Case Study: Renson (Belgium)

Renson, a family business headquartered in Waregem, Belgium, was founded in 1909 by Polydor Renson to manufacture steel hardware for windows and doors. Polydor's great-grandson, Paul Renson, has led the company since 1982. During this time, Renson expanded into the design and production of solar shading, ventilation systems, and outdoor living spaces including carports, porches, and pergolas made from lightweight aluminum.

After years of focusing on new product development for European markets, Renson looked to grow through international expansion. It had been selling to a few U.S. architects from its Belgian office, but it realized it needed a U.S. outpost for the world's largest market. It needed to let U.S. customers know that Renson was committed to doing business here.

In 2012, Paul Renson sent a young business development executive, Gilles Vanpoucke, to build the U.S. business. The first thing Gilles did was to incorporate Renson's U.S. subsidiary in the state of Delaware, based on the advice of U.S. lawyers (Chapter 7 explains why Delaware is the top choice for incorporation). The business entity was quickly set up through a local certified public accountant (CPA), and the CPA's office was the company's first U.S. address.[26]

Gilles was tasked with choosing the location for the U.S. business. Since most competitors were on the East Coast, he thought it would be advantageous to set up shop on the West Coast. He focused on California, because of the revenue and growth potential, and he selected Los Angeles for the company's first U.S. office. Not only was L.A. close to several big real estate markets that offered attractive housing and cultural options, it was also a major hub for shipping and air travel.

(*continued*)

(*continued*)

Next, Gilles and the team in Belgium had to choose which of its many products to introduce. Renson couldn't reconfigure and adjust its entire product line. Technical requirements are different in the United States, such as the use of 120-volt power lines versus Europe's 230-volt, and U.S. building permits required different certifications than European ones. Documentation needed to be localized, and price lists needed to be in U.S. dollars. Renson's team decided to concentrate on their high-end, outdoor living products. These products' innovative design and detailed construction would differentiate them in the market. Plus, architects, builders, and their wealthy clients were more concerned with quality than price.

Lastly, Gilles had to decide which channels it would use to sell and distribute its products. The option of building a large salesforce was too expensive and would take too long to establish. Instead, he decided to work with qualified dealers who could provide expert advice, installation, and customer service. Gilles referred to these dealers as partners and "local heroes who really knew the local markets." In addition, Renson would need a few of its own salespeople to handle the intercompany transactions with its Belgian parent company before selling the Renson products to the dealers. This internal exchange would result in lower import duties for U.S. buyers, too.

Later Renson created offices in the Northeast, Central U.S., and Florida in addition to Los Angeles to manage the dealers in each region. In 2018, Renson opened a production facility in Dallas, Texas. Gilles said, "I'm proud we were able to establish a U.S. business and start producing here within five years. I think the difference is we created a U.S. business rather than being a European export."

Lessons from This Case Study

1. **Establish a U.S. business entity.** Renson couldn't grow its business when it treated the United States as an export market. By establishing a U.S. subsidiary, it was able to convince partners and customers alike that it was a serious player in the market.
2. **Carefully select product categories.** Renson smartly chose the premium outdoor living category where it could be most competitive. It also minimized the cost, complexity, and time to enter the U.S. market by focusing on a limited number of products.
3. **Localize products and marketing materials.** Renson reconfigured its products and secured certifications to meet U.S. building requirements. It also revised its marketing materials and product documentation to American language and metrics.
4. **Select a beachhead market.** Renson did not have the resources to compete in every U.S. region. It selected the promising West Coast market to enter first. After gaining traction and a solid reputation, it expanded to other regions of the country.

Notes

1. Conversation with Federico Tozzi, executive director of the Italy-American Chamber of Commerce, on February 5, 2021
2. A.G. Lafley and Roger Martin, *Playing to Win: How Strategy Really Works* (Boston, Massachusetts: Harvard Business Review Press, 2013) p. 58.
3. Member News, "3 Important Facts International Businesses Need to Know About Sales Taxes," French-American Chamber of Commerce, February 2, 2021, www.faccnyc.org/news/3-important-facts-international-businesses-need-know-about-sales-tax
4. Colin Woodard, "Up in Arms," Tufts Now, January 24, 2014, now.tufts.edu/articles/arms
5. "Transcript: Jamelle Bouie Interviews Woody Holton for 'The Ezra Klein Show,'" The New York Times Podcasts, October 19, 2021, www.nytimes.com/2021/10/19/podcasts/transcript-ezra-klein-interviews-woody-holton.html

6. Colin Woodard, *American Nations* (New York, New York: Penguin Books, 2011).
7. Colin Woodard, "Up in Arms," Tufts Now, January 24, 2014, now.tufts .edu/articles/arms
8. Ibid.
9. Ibid.
10. Ibid.
11. Ibid.
12. Ibid.
13. Ibid.
14. Conversation with Tobias Reisner, co-founder and Global Partner of HDT International, on February 3, 2021
15. Conversation with Surein de Silva Wijeyeratne, head of Corporate Communications at MAS Holdings, on April 20, 2021
16. MAS Acme, MAS Holdings website, Accessed February 15, 2021, www .masholdings.com/americas
17. Joe White, "How and when to raise venture capital from Silicon Valley—for European and Asian startups," Medium, August 1, 2019, medium.com/entrepreneur-first/how-and-when-to-raise-venture-capital-from-silicon-valley-for-european-and-asian-startups-dd27037c1d1b
18. SelectUSA website, www.trade.gov/selectusa-home
19. "Q4 2020: Priciest U.S. Office Submarkets," CommercialSearch (blog), February 9,2021, www.commercialsearch.com/blog/50-most-expensive-u-s-office-submarkets-q4-2020
20. "OECD Labour Force Statistics 2020," OECD, Accessed December 4, 2021, www.oecd-ilibrary.org/employment/oecd-labour-force-statistics-2020_5842cc7f-en
21. Clusters 101 | U.S. Cluster Mapping, accessed April 05, 2021, www .clustermapping.us/content/clusters-101
22. Conversation with Suzanne Southard, president of Swedish Women Educational Association International, on October 18, 2021
23. Jeff Andrews, "Zumper National Rent Report," The Zumper Blog (blog), September 27, 2021, www.zumper.com/blog/rental-price-data
24. Bonne Maman press release, "Premium Preserves Brand Bonne Maman® Launches First U.S. Digital TV Ad Campaign, Global Newswire, April 12, 2021, www.globenewswire.com/news-2021/04/12
25. Progressive Grocer, "Number of supermarket stores in the United States from 2013 to 2018, by operator," Chart, April 1, 2019, Statista, Accessed April 17, 2022, www-statista-com/statistics/240920/number-of-us-supermarket-stores-by-operator
26. Conversation with Gilles Vanpouke, vice president and senior business development manager of Renson, on September 28, 2021

7

Make It Legal

Before attempting to enter the United States with your business or trying to start one here, you need to know some basic principles and practices of American corporate law and legal systems. The U.S. legal system is complicated, extensive, and uniquely different from those found in other countries. Getting the legal stuff right at the start will save you costly problems later. Also, it will impact your ability to raise capital and scale your business.

> "I saw the legal system close up, and I understood that it was built by lawyers for lawyers," said Shari Redstone, chairperson of Paramount Global, after a messy succession fight for the company her father started. "And unless you have an attorney to navigate it, you're not going to be successful."[1]

Since I am not an attorney, I am not giving you any legal advice. My goal is to provide a general overview of the U.S. legal environment and to highlight issues you might consider. That way you can develop questions and topics to discuss with qualified lawyers, accountants, and other business advisors. I cannot overstate how crucially important it is that you engage qualified professionals who have experience in U.S. markets. They can guide you on specific legal and tax considerations affecting your business decisions, and they'll often share their experiences regarding how those business decisions might play out. (See the "Legal Checklist" in Appendix C to help prepare for these discussions.)

In this chapter, I'll focus on how the U.S. system is different and why it developed that way. Then I'll cover issues that are particularly important for U.S. entry and expansion, followed by brief overviews of things like trademarks and patents.

Quirks of the U.S. Legal System

Every country has laws to regulate what individuals and businesses can and can't do. Every country has a court system for interpreting and enforcing those laws. And every country has judges who make decisions about the law—often settling disputes between competing parties of individuals, organizations, and groups of people. While these truths certainly apply to the United States, its legal system has fundamental differences that make it difficult for many non-U.S. nationals to understand and follow.

Common Law vs. Civil Law. The United States has a common law system, which is fundamentally different from civil law systems typically found in most Asian, Continental European, Latin American, and Scandinavian nations. Civil law systems trace back to the Roman Civilization and the Napoleonic Code commissioned by the French emperor around 1800. Civil law nations have comprehensive laws that are codified or systematically arranged to avoid overlapping with one another or creating inconsistencies. Judges make rulings based on their interpretation of these written laws without any obligation to follow what other judges have decided in similar cases. A jury of citizens might or might not be involved, depending on the country and type of case.

Common law systems, on the other hand, which the United States relies on, were created by English kings in the Middle Ages to extend their authority over conquered lands. Appointed judges acted as surrogates for the king and determined each case based on its merits. Besides England and the United States, other common law countries include Australia, Canada, India,

Israel, Pakistan, and Singapore. Today, instead of acting on behalf of a monarchy, common law judges act on behalf of the people.

Common law systems are often called case law or judge-made law, because rulings are based on decisions from earlier cases in addition to the written laws. Judges, sometimes along with a jury of citizens, listen in court to the arguments presented by lawyers representing each of the opposing parties in a particular case. Along with identifying legal precedents from similar previous cases, the lawyers on each side might call on various witnesses or experts and question them in court. The judge and jury then take some time to evaluate the arguments and evidence to determine their verdict. The quality of crafted arguments and legal evidence presented have a great deal of influence on the final outcome and decision. Note that because common law lawyers spend a considerable amount of time researching and preparing for each court case, legal costs in the United States are generally higher than in civil law systems.

Multitiered and Complex. The U.S. legal system is complicated in both the way it creates the laws and how it decides them. Laws are created at the multiple levels of national, state, county, and local municipalities. Federal statutes are laws created and passed by elected members of the U.S. Congress, usually with the approval of the elected U.S. president. Each of the 50 states—plus the District of Columbia, Guam, Puerto Rico, and the U.S. Virgin Islands—has a congressional legislature that creates state laws. Counties and municipalities within each state also enact laws, often called *ordinances*, that apply to everyone within their jurisdiction. In cases where there is some kind of contradiction or controversy regarding a judicial ruling, then the U.S. federal laws overrule state laws, and state laws overrule municipal laws. That hierarchy of law allows the United States to maintain some level of order.

The U.S. legal landscape is further complicated by its dual-court judicial system of federal and state courts. (The state court system includes municipal/city and local courts.) Within each system are trial courts and appellate courts. Trial courts decide on disputes and criminal cases based on evidence and the application of legal principles. Appellate courts (sometimes called Courts of Appeals) decide whether the law was applied correctly in trial courts and, in some cases, whether a particular law is "constitutional" (i.e., whether it aligns with the U.S. Constitution). The federal system has 94 district or trial courts, 13 courts of appeal, and a single powerful U.S. Supreme Court.

Another complication in the U.S. system is the segmentation of lawyers. Lawyers have to be granted permission to practice law in each state and federal territory. Permission is granted after the candidate has graduated from an approved law school and has passed a state's bar examination. A lawyer who is admitted to one state's bar is not automatically allowed to practice elsewhere, although some states have reciprocity agreements. In addition, because of the breadth and complexity of laws and regulations, lawyers tend to specialize in specific areas, such as intellectual property or employment law.

Why So Litigious?

The United States is considered more litigious than virtually every other country. To people from other countries, the U.S. legal system seems chaotic and full of frivolous lawsuits and court cases. For example, the Kellogg Company had to fight three lawsuits for deceptive marketing of its Pop-Tarts toaster pastries. In a 2020 class action lawsuit, the plaintiffs' attorney charged, "Whole Grain Frosted Strawberry Toasted Pastries is a false, deceptive, and misleading name because it contains mostly nonstrawberry fruit ingredients." The case asked for $5 million in relief.[2]

The main reason why there are so many lawsuits in the United States is because of its legal system's unique treatment of penalties and costs. In most countries, you pay the other party's legal fees when you lose a lawsuit. This deters people from filing lawsuits they might not win. But in the United States, parties pay only their own lawyers' fees. In many cases, losers don't pay anything if their lawyers agreed that their payment would be contingent on winning. Some companies and wealthy individuals file lawsuits just to see if the other side will settle out of court quickly, rather than incur expensive legal fees.

So, when an American says, "I'll sue you," there is a good chance they will. That said, let's look at the ways that you can gain legal protections in the United States, such as by creating a business entity.

Establishing Business Entities

The U.S. legal system is generally known for being pro-businesses. In fact, corporations have similar legal rights as people do—a legal notion called *corporate personhood*. Corporations can enter contracts and fight legal battles, separately from its owners, managers, and employees. The U.S. Supreme Court even confirmed in 2010 that corporations had First Amendment rights for free speech.[3]

Therefore, establishing a formal U.S. business "entity" (company, corporation, LLC, etc.) should be your first step for most U.S. expansions. Of course, you might wonder if that step is really necessary if you're currently exporting products into the United States through a local distributor or online marketplace. But the fact is, at some point, establishing a U.S. company will be necessary and essential in order to maximize revenue and to secure legal protection.

Several people asked if a foreigner (an individual) can create a U.S. business entity. The answer is "yes." You don't have to be a U.S. citizen or a permanent resident or even have a work permit to form a legal business entity. Foreign companies can form U.S. business entities, too. These are known as *subsidiaries*, which are divisions owned by a company that is headquartered outside of the United States.

In addition, non-U.S. nationals can own shares, sit on the board of directors, and work at U.S. companies. However, being an owner, board member, or employee of a U.S. business does not automatically allow a foreigner to actually *work* in the United

States. I'll cover employment and visa issues more fully in Chapter 10. For now, let's take a closer look at the reasons for establishing a U.S. business entity: to maximize growth, reduce risk, and increase your business's attractiveness to investors.

Maximize Revenue and Growth. U.S. companies prefer to do business with other U.S. companies; they believe it is safer and easier. To work with foreign entities, therefore, American executives want to see long-term commitment to the U.S. market from the international player. This is particularly true where product upgrades translate into multiyear relationships. Establishing a U.S. subsidiary demonstrates this commitment. The software developer Rokt established a U.S. subsidiary soon after proving that its ecommerce optimization software worked in Australia. That led to securing several large U.S. clients, including Disney, Staples, and Vistaprint. (See the case study at the end of Chapter 2.)

Moreover, U.S. business entities scale faster since deals close more quickly and smoothly than with non-U.S. businesses. American businesspeople often insist that any contracts between their company and a foreign entity be written according to U.S. law. Their in-house legal and procurement departments prefer U.S. contracts, because the legal language and terms are more familiar. If there are disputes, they don't want to go to another country's court to settle the case.

Reduce Risk. A U.S. business entity provides valuable legal protection that reduces the risk of doing business. International companies are attractive targets for lawsuits and legal threats. Unscrupulous companies and individuals try to tap into the assets of non-U.S. organizations, because they think international executives will settle quickly due to their unfamiliarity with U.S. laws and court system. If you've created a U.S. business entity, however, the assets of your foreign parent company will generally be shielded from financial liabilities and legal attacks. In many cases, such a move will also protect the personal assets of investors, directors, and officers.

Let's say you open a showroom in Miami and a delivery person slips and falls, requiring expensive hospitalization. If you've been wise and have set up a U.S. subsidiary, the delivery company and the harmed individual would, in almost all cases, bring a lawsuit only against the assets of your U.S. business entity—not against your whole company. But if the Miami showroom is only just a branch store or office, the delivery company could sue the international company for a much larger amount. In other words, the subsidiary provides a level of insulation to the parent company.

Increase Attractiveness to Investors. U.S. business entities tap into the world's largest and most diverse pool of investor money to fund their expansion. (You'll learn more about U.S. financing options in Chapter 8.) Most top U.S. investors feel safer investing in U.S. companies because they can better assess the risks and external factors. The investors' lawyers can better anticipate the legal and regulatory issues for U.S. business entities.

Since startups and scale-ups can grow quickly in U.S. markets, your business could potentially earn huge financial gains. Investors say the United States offers a clear path to exit—going public or being bought—with a big payout. Remember, however, that successful investments are only hypothetical, paper profits until the investor sells their shares. Following an initial public offering (IPO) of a business entity, an investor may sell shares to the public, subject to certain restrictions. The United States happens to have the two largest stock markets in the world, and they attract the most IPOs: the New York Stock Exchange (NYSE) and the Nasdaq Stock Market (NASDAQ).

An even quicker path to a rewarding exit is when the startup or scale-up is bought by a bigger company, which is relatively routine when the acquisition is another U.S. business entity. Google, now Alphabet, has spent $19 billion acquiring more than 225 companies.[4] The Coca-Cola Company has spent more than $9.4 billion acquiring consumer companies, including Mexican Topo-Chico S.A. and Australian Organic & Raw Trading Company.[5]

Types of Business Entities

There are a number of business structures in the United States, but only two—C corporation (C corp) and limited liability company (LLC)—are appropriate for international businesses and entrepreneurs. There are also proprietorships and general partnerships, but these don't provide owners or members any personal protection. Another type of legal entity, S corporation, doesn't allow non-U.S. citizens to have any share of ownership. (Also see Figure 7.1 Business entities chart.)

C Corporation. The C corp is a legal entity that can hire employees, borrow money, issue securities, hold intellectual property, pursue lawsuits, and enter contracts. Legally, it owns

	C Corp	LLC
Owners	Shareholders	Members
Ownership	Ownership allocated by number of shares	Ownership can be divided by members as they see fit
Governance	Governed by Directors	Governed by Members
Documents to Form	Articles of Incorporation, Certificate of Incorporation	Articles of Organization, Certificate of Organization
Tax	Considered separate legal entity and pays corporate income taxes on profits	Business does not pay taxes, as passes through profits and tax obligation to members
Meetings	Annual meeting required for interested shareholders	No requirements for meetings
Protections	Shareholders and directors not liable for corporation's debts or liabilities	Members are not liable for LLC's debts or liabilities
Other	Certain retirement plans, stock option and employee stock purchase plans available only for C Corps	

(Based on chart in Octopus Ventures, "Question the Questions" report, 2018)

Figure 7.1 Business Entity Comparison

the assets, including purchased equipment and buildings, as well as the liabilities of the business. If the C corp is involved in several lines of business, it can create separate subsidiaries to isolate the assets and liabilities of each business.

C corps can be owned by individuals, partnerships, trusts, or other entities, including corporations. The amount, or percentage, owned is determined by the number of shares each party holds. Shareholders are able to sell and trade shares to any buyer at any price, generally without the approval of other shareholders. When C corps hold their annual meetings, that is where shareholders can ask questions and bring up policy and other issues.

Management and investment decisions are made by the board of directors elected by shareholders. Directors rely on executives within the corporation, known as *officers*, to carry out their decisions. Directors owe fiduciary duties to the shareholders, as well as "duty of care" and "duty of loyalty" obligations to act in the best interest of the corporation. Importantly, the shareholders, directors, and officers are not personally responsible for any debts, obligations, or claims against the C corp. (However, there are rare cases when individuals at the corporation engage in fraud, fail to pay wages, or misuse funds—and in those cases the individual can be held responsible.)

C corps may be required to pay federal, state, and local taxes on profits. Tax documents and filings are usually made by an outside accounting firm and subject to independent audits at larger, more mature companies. Directors of the C corp can choose to distribute after-tax profits to shareholders as dividends. However, these distributions become part of the shareholder's individual income, which results in a double taxation.

B Corporation. B corps have the same legal characteristics and benefits of C corporations. The distinction is these for-profit companies have been awarded a certification of social and environmental performance. Directors of B corps are able to consider other stakeholders when making decisions, as their missions include generating a public benefit. (The Danish company Too Good to Go, presented as a case study in Chapter 4, is a B corp.) Venture capitalists and angel investors generally view the B corp as a marketing designation.[6]

Limited Liability Company. The LLC structure is a blend of a partnership and a corporation. It was first introduced in a few U.S. states in the 1970s, mostly modeled after the German GmbH business structure. LLCs are a popular choice for small businesses, consulting firms, and service organizations. They are frequently used for real estate deals, too. In fact, there are more LLCs in the United States than any other type of business entity. Limited liability companies are relatively fast, inexpensive, and easy to set up. My own consulting firm, Rocket Market Development, was formed as an LLC in 2014. It was created in one day with legal and filing fees that totaled less than $1,000.

Here are several things that you should know about LLCs:

- Similar to corporations, LLCs can be owned by individuals, partnerships, trusts, or other entities, including corporations.
- An LLC can be owned by foreign individuals and companies.
- LLC owners are called members. Their share of ownership is more flexible than corporations, since capital contributions, if required, can be in cash, property, or services. It's up to the members to decide how to divide the equity.
- An LLC does not pay federal income taxes. If structured properly, it also will not pay state and local taxes.
- Similar to partnerships and sole proprietorships, the profits and losses of an LLC get passed to the owner members. These individuals then report it on their personal income tax filings.
- LLCs give its members significant protection from liability and debts. If your LLC gets sued, your personal assets can't be taken away. If the LLC goes bankrupt, the owners (or members) don't have to pay the business debts from their personal funds.

While an LLC is a viable option, a C corp is generally a better platform for growth and raising venture capital. VCs and angel investors don't like the LLC business structure because there is no easy way to divide or sell ownership. Also, there is no easy way to give options to employees and advisors.[7]

When Is It Time to Establish a Business Entity?

Many international companies create a U.S. business entity upon hiring its first U.S. employee. Even if it moves an employee from the company's home country to the United States, the company will need to pay U.S. employment taxes. This situation can get messy, as the employee could be subject to taxes in both countries. To avoid double payment of taxes, international companies will need to set up a U.S. business entity.

In Chapter 6, you read how Renson created its C corp when it set up a U.S. sales organization. Another Belgian company, Proxyclick, formed its U.S. business entity when it hired local client service representatives for its visitor management software.

Another trigger point for establishing a U.S. business entity is when there are significant sales revenues. International companies should separate their U.S. and non-U.S. income for tax purposes, as corporate tax rates are different for each country. Prior to tax reforms in 2017, the United States had one of the highest rates with nearly 40 percent of taxable income, which was triple the rate in Ireland. Currently, in 2021, the United States corporate tax rate is 26 percent, still double the rate in Ireland.[8] Tax rates will undoubtedly fluctuate again, which is another reason to keep your U.S. and non-U.S. businesses separate.

Startups should investigate company-as-a-service platforms, such as Gust Launch, that make the process of incorporation easy, fast, and inexpensive. Founders can set up a Delaware C corp in days, receive a federal tax identification number (EIN), and issue stock in just days. In addition, these platforms offer tools to manage startups' legal, financial, and operational needs.

Where Do You Establish Your Business?

This decision would be easy if there was a United States C corp or a national LLC legal structure. Instead, business entities must be formed in one of the 50 states or the District of Columbia. The choice doesn't have to be where the business offices are located or where the employees reside. In other words, *you* can decide where to form your business entity. Why? Because each state has its own laws and requirements about creating and operating businesses. There are different filing fees and processes for each state, too.

If you plan to attract outside investors and possibly sell shares, then you'll probably want to create it in Delaware, which is home to 60 percent of the 500 largest U.S. companies.[9] Delaware has a well-established, business-friendly court system and tax code. Delaware laws are considered flexible and offer greater privacy, particularly for structuring corporations and boards of directors. The big investment firms prefer Delaware because their lawyers are familiar with its statutes and processes, so legal documents are processed and reviewed faster in complex transactions. Nevada, South Dakota, and Wyoming are also considered good choices, because those states impose no corporate or individual income tax.[10]

International startups and scale-ups might consider conducting a "Delaware Flip," by making your newly formed Delaware C corp into the new "parent" company with a stock swap with existing shareholders of the foreign company. The foreign company then becomes a wholly owned subsidiary of the Delaware C corp, and the larger entity can attract more investors. The possible tax consequences of a Delaware Flip are very complex, so if you decide to do it, it is essential that you involve the services of expert tax advisors and lawyers.

If you are not looking for investors or an eventual sale of your company, then choosing Delaware probably isn't important. Several business and legal experts recommend establishing your C corp or LLC in the state where you do the most business or where your U.S. headquarters is located. Then you would avoid the added approximate $500 yearly expense of maintaining a registered agent and paying reporting fees and franchise tax in a second state.[11]

Intellectual Property Protection

The U.S. legal system offers protection for intellectual property (IP), which refers to intangible creations of the mind that can be legally protected. These IP laws were established by Congress to encourage innovation by providing incentives to create new works and generate useful inventions. Specifically, IP laws prevent unauthorized use or copying of your inventions, formulas, creative work, and brands. In the United States, any infringement on others' intellectual property could result in a costly lawsuit and possibly your company or product being shut out of the market. (See the case study at the end of this chapter, which recounts how Pillow Partners experienced trademark and other legal issues when it entered the U.S. market.)

For international companies and entrepreneurs, exclusive IP rights are a valuable asset for both growing business and securing investors in the United States. Note, however, that intellectual property ownership in another country doesn't guarantee ownership in the United States. Ownership is granted by the U.S. Patent and Trademark Office (USPTO) of the U.S. Department of Commerce, which checks there are no similar trademarks, service marks, or patents already owned by someone else. Original works of authorship, however—such as computer codes, books, songs, plays, artworks, architectural designs—operate under copyright law, which I describe below, along with the two other forms of legal IP protection available in the United States: trademarks and patents.

Trademarks and Service Marks. A trademark is a brand identifier for a product. It can be a word phrase, logo, or design that marks the product and differentiates it from competitors. For example, the Nike name, its "swoosh" graphic symbol, and the "Just Do It" phrase are all trademarks. A service mark is similar to a trademark, although it is used to identify services rather than products. United Airlines and its "Fly the Friendly Skies" tagline and globe logo are service marks because air travel is a service.

Trademark and service mark rights are determined by being either the first to use the mark or the first to register it with the USPTO. To claim the first use, the symbol ™ (which stands for unregistered trademark) should appear immediately after the brand name or logo. That symbol provides some immediate protection under common law rights. However, simply placing a ™ symbol on your brand doesn't fully protect you if someone infringes on your trademark and claims it for their own brand—and the amount of money you can recoup is limited. Therefore, it is best to *register* the trademark, which is relatively inexpensive and easily done online with the USPTO. Once the trademark is registered, you should switch to using the ® ("registered") symbol.

Before you invest in creating a brand name or logo and certainly before you try to register your product or service, first check for similar trademarks and service markets. You can do a preliminary check of a brand, service, or product name's availability on the USPTO's TESS website. The database doesn't list nonregistered trademarks or state registered trademarks, however, so a more comprehensive search should be conducted before investing in a brand name or design. LegalZoom and other online legal technology companies offer this service for a few hundred dollars. The USPTO recommends speaking with a U.S.-licensed attorney who specializes in trademark law to guide you through the application process.

Patents and Trade Secrets. A patent is a right granted that excludes others from making, selling, or using an invention or discovery. Patent protection is both a competitive advantage and an attractive asset for investors. However, the process to secure a patent is demanding and the cost is significant. It requires skilled experts to prepare and substantiate the claims in a patent application. The process can take up to two years, although you can pay an extra fee to get a priority examination in 6 to 12 months. Also, you can file a provisional application to receive "Patent Pending" status for 12 months.

There are three types of U.S. patents. The first, called a *utility patent*, is granted for useful inventions and discoveries. This category includes machines, manufactured items, business processes, software, and pharmaceuticals. These patents give the owner exclusive right to use the invention for 20 years. The second type, *design patents*, covers nonfunctional, ornamental designs, typically on a product or package. Apple iPhone, Oakley sunglasses, the curvy Coca-Cola bottle, and computer emojis have been awarded design patents. Design patents provide protection for 15 years from the date granted. The last type is a *plant patent* for the invention or discovery of a new variety of asexually reproducing plant.

The timing for launching products and securing patents is important to investors. Particularly for a startup, investors will want to know who owns the IP. In many European and other countries, inventions created by an employee are automatically owned by the company. But in the United States, inventions are owned by the individual inventor unless they assign the IP to the company. This assignment must be in writing, and it is often done in their employment or contractor agreement.

Since patents are disclosed to the public in the application process, some companies have chosen to keep them as a "trade secret." Coca-Cola chose to keep secret its formula for its famous beverage rather than apply for a patent. Also, patents last for only 20 years and cannot be renewed after that time. Therefore, this is a strategic business decision. Just know that it is perfectly legal to reverse-engineer and copy a trade secret if you can figure it out.[12]

Certainly, any questions or issues about patents and IP should be discussed with a U.S.-based attorney that specializes in your industry. This is especially important because U.S. patent law is continually undergoing changes in several areas, including what types of inventions are eligible for patents.

Copyrights. Copyrights provide the creators of "original works of authorship" exclusive rights to reproduce, display, and distribute it. These original works can be books, computer code, music, paintings, movies, and pieces of sculpture and architecture. Not included under copyright law, however, are things like ideas, processes, systems, or methods of operation.

Unlike a patent or trademark, the author doesn't need to apply to a government agency to obtain a copyright. It goes into effect when the work is created and fixed in a tangible medium, such as printed on paper or recorded in a computer file. However, to bring a lawsuit for copyright infringement of an authored work in U.S. federal court, authors must have registered their copyright with the U.S. Copyright Office. For most works, copyrights stay in effect a full 70 years after the author has died.

Therefore, you should mark all original work, such as books and artwork, with © and the year it was created to show it is copyright protected.

As I mentioned at the start of this chapter, the U.S. legal system is complicated, and you should enlist counsel in the form of a qualified lawyer before attempting to navigate it. Appendix C provides a checklist that will help you identify the necessary legal steps and prepare questions to ask legal and tax experts.

In the next chapter, I will focus on the important topic of financing your U.S. expansion and new ventures. Let's first look at an interesting case about a U.K. company that encountered legal complications.

Case Study: Pillow Partners (Scotland)

This case study recounts how a promising U.K. company successfully navigated tricky legal waters on its journey to the U.S. market. It was established in 2015 in Ayrshire,

Scotland, under the name Pillow Property Partners Ltd. Founder Scott Weir originally had named his company simply "Pillow" until he ran into legal issues. Before we examine that story, however, let's look at the background of the company and its remarkable founder.

The company provides a service that connects short-term renters (defined as one day to one year) with property owners through a combination of digital technology and dedicated support people. Renters are assigned local concierges, and property owners receive marketing, logistics, and other management services. In addition, the company contributes to local businesses, charities, and good causes on behalf of its customers. One way it does this is by requiring property owners to donate either the rental space or equivalent monetary value of up to seven days per year. Renters are also offered the opportunity to donate 1 percent to 3 percent of the rental fee to charity.

From its base in Ayrshire, the company quickly expanded to Glasgow and then throughout Scotland. In 2018 it expanded into England and Wales, focusing on holiday homes, serviced apartments, B&Bs, and hotels. Within four years Pillow Property Partners had grown into a multimillion-pound business with more than 1,000 properties under management.

In January 2022, it opened a U.S. office in Miami with the goal of replicating its U.K. business model of short-term rental management with a community social-impact element. It saw additional possibilities in the United States for B2B marketing and software-as-a-service (SaaS) revenue. Florida was chosen because of its sizable vacation market, business-friendly political environment, and numerous venture capital investors.

(*continued*)

(*continued*)

Not Your Typical Founder

Scott Weir became a landlord at the age of 17, and he established his first property management company in his early 20s. He had big plans, which he nurtured while getting a master of business administration (MBA). In 2016 Scott started Pillow Property Partners Ltd and was named Ayrshire's Entrepreneur of the Year. Scott won Scotland's Startup Summit competition in 2018, winning the prize money of £20,000 and a place in FutureX's Silicon Valley Accelerator program. More awards followed: Scott was named as the Small Business Great British Entrepreneur in 2019, and the Scottish government funded his study of entrepreneurship at Babson College in Massachusetts.

As Scott said, "Being in the residential lettings market for more than two decades, I have seen that sector change massively. These changes, mixed in with technological advances and shifting customer demographics, meant that it was the ideal time to launch Pillow. Five years earlier and it would not have been possible, and a few years later and we would have had a massive challenge in a saturated market."[13]

Scott's seize-the-moment enthusiasm was seen as bold and courageous by some. But others—such as Ian Houston, president of the Scottish Business Network Americas—expected nothing less from him as a Scot. As Ian proudly proclaimed, "Scottish history is full of bold characters who took risks; today is no different. Scots continue to contribute directly to the modern economic and cultural landscape."[14]

When business came to a standstill during the 2020 pandemic, Scott spent the lockdown researching, networking, and preparing for U.S. expansion. The government organizations Scottish Enterprise and GlobalScot connected him to U.S.-based Scottish executives and consultants. He entered two accelerator programs, WEVE Acceleration and Newchip, where he met with mentors and experts in U.S. law, employment, and business. At WEVE, he met Scott Smesdresman, partner at Brown Rudnick LLP, who gave a seminar on forming U.S. entities. (Despite his first name, Smesdresman has no Scottish heritage.) Later the two "Scotts" met to discuss this and other legal topics.

Avoiding a Legal Snafu

Before entering the U.S. market, Scott Weir needed to create a separate U.S. business entity. It was necessary to process legal requirements for federal and state taxes for employees, and it didn't matter they planned to have U.K. citizens on work visas in the United States. Creating a U.S. entity would keep its income separate from the parent company for tax purposes. The company didn't want to risk having to pay taxes for U.S. revenue in both countries.

Numerous mentors and lawyers advised Scott to form a C corporation. They said venture capitalists (VCs) wouldn't consider other formats, and that was an important consideration since the company needed to raise money. They told him to "incorporate in Delaware for legal reasons" to do with clarity, simplicity, and predictability. The state has the reputation for its business-friendly legal and court system and preference in the investment community. And so, in November 2020, the company incorporated in Delaware as Pillow Partners.[15]

While the U.K. company's full legal name was Pillow Property Partners Ltd, in the U.K. it had been calling itself "Pillow" for training and marketing purposes. It had a full EU trademark for the name Pillow, too. However, the EU trademark *didn't have any legal weight in the United*

(*continued*)

(*continued*)

States, and Scott already had learned of a potential trademark-infringement issue.

Expedia, a Microsoft spinoff with $6 billion annual revenues, had purchased a software company in 2018 called Pillow—"a software solution that helps building owners and managers empower their long-term residents to rent their residences."[16] When Scott Weir's company was hoping to use the name in the United States, in 2020, however, Expedia had closed its Pillow operation in an effort to cut costs during the COVID crisis. Even though the name Pillow had essentially been abandoned and was considered somewhat generic, Scott decided it wasn't worth the legal cost and nuisance to do battle for a trademark on that particular name. In the end, he decided to pursue a safer trademark—Pillow Partners—for the U.S. market.

Scott reported that, overall, the U.S. legal environment was more complex than he expected.[17] He hadn't realized how each state, and often each city, had different regulations. He also found that navigating the U.S. system was a lot more expensive than in the United Kingdom, even for simple document creation or advice. Still, he tells other international entrepreneurs: "Do not be put off by these things. Having good people on the ground as advisors and mentors will make things possible."

Lessons from This Case Study

1. **Set up U.S. business entity.** Establishing a C corporation in the United States provides both ease of doing business and legal protection. It's essential when hiring U.S. employees for federal and state tax purposes.

2. **U.S. trademarks are required.** Trademarks and patents are country specific. Failure to secure trademark rights in the United States could lead to expensive lawsuits and potential blockage from doing business.
3. **The United States is a litigious country.** People will sue in the United States just because they have the money to hire the best lawyers. Therefore, lawyers play an important role in anticipating potential problems and navigating the U.S. legal system.
4. **Connections are important.** Scott met capable lawyers and others through introductions from people at U.S. accelerators and various Scottish organizations. These connections were valuable in getting established in the U.S. market quickly.

Notes

1. "Shari Redstone Quotes," BrainyQuote.com, BrainyMedia Inc, 2022, Accessed May 3, 2022, www.brainyquote.com/quotes/shari_redstone_874524
2. Jesse Newman and Jennifer Calfas, "Are There Enough Strawberries in a Strawberry Pop-Tart? A Court Might Decide," *The Wall Street Journal*, October 25, 2021, www.wsj.com/articles/are-there-enough-strawberries-in-a-strawberry-pop-tart-a-court-might-decide-11635207549
3. Renee Montagne, "When Did Companies Become People?" NPR, July 28, 2014, www.npr.org/transcripts/335288388
4. "Google Acquisitions," Microacquire, Accessed May 3, 2022, acquiredby.co/google-acquisitions/
5. "Acquisitions by The Coca-Cola Company," Tracxn, Accessed May 3, 2022, tracxn.com/d/acquisitions/acquisitionsbyThe-Coca-Cola-Company
6. David S. Rose, *The Startup Checklist* (Hoboken, NJ: John Wiley & Sons, Inc., 2016), p. 88.
7. Ibid.
8. Sean Bray, "Corporate Tax Rates around the World," Tax Foundation, December 9, 2021, taxfoundation.org/publications/corporate-tax-rates-around-the-world
9. "What is the Best State to Incorporate In?" IncNow, April 26, 2022, www.incnow.com/blog/2022/04/26/best-state-to-incorporate/

10. Erik York and Jared Walczak, "State and Local Tax Burdens, Calendar Year 2022, Tax Foundation, April 7, 2022, taxfoundation.org/center/state-tax-policy
11. Nellie Akap, "Pros and Cons of Incorporating in Delaware," Entrepreneur, Accessed September 30, 2021, www.entrepreneur.com/article/287677
12. Orly Lobel, "Filing for a Patent versus Keeping Your Invention a Trade Secret," *Harvard Business Review*, November 21, 2013, hbr.org/2013/11/filing-for-a-patent-versus-keeping-your-invention-a-trade-secret
13. Timeline, "Scott Weir Will Travel to the U.S.as Part of the FutureX Silicon Valley Accelerate Programme," Accessed December 27, 2021, pillowpartners.co.uk/ceo-scott-weir-will-travel-to-the-us-as-part-of-the-futurex-silicon-valley-accelerate-programme
14. Conversation with Ian Houston, president of Scottish Business Network, on February 22, 2022
15. Conversation with Scott Weir, founder and CEO of Pillow Partners, on January 8, 2022
16. "Expedia Group Acquires Pillow and ApartmentJet to Enhance Its Alternative Accommodations Marketplace for Residents, Owners and Managers in Urban Markets," Expedia Brand MediaRoom, Accessed December 27, 2021, newsroom.expedia.com/2018-10-25-Expedia-Group-Acquires-Pillow-and-ApartmentJet-to-Enhance-Its-Alternative-Accommodations-Marketplace-for-Residents-Owners-and-Managers-in-Urban-Markets
17. Conversation with Scott Weir, founder and CEO of Pillow Partners, on January 8, 2022

8

Financing U.S. Expansion

Let's talk about money, or, as it's more formally known, capital. More than half the international businesspeople and entrepreneurs who I surveyed for this book thought securing capital would be the biggest obstacle to U.S. expansion. Several international executives had delayed their launch plans until capital was raised. One was dealing with an immediate need for funds to pay for a newly expanded office and additional staff. The stress and pressure were causing them to feel distressed and panicked.

> "Cash is the lifeblood of your business," said Robert Herjavec, Canadian businessman; born in Yugoslavia and best known for his role on the television series Shark Tank. "There are very few things in business that will kill you, but running out of cash is one of those things. You can recover from almost any other mistake, but if you run out of cash, you're dead."[1]

Fortunately, there is plenty of cash available and a plethora of providers in the world's largest economy. The U.S. banking system has $18 trillion in assets, which is greater than the gross domestic product (GDP) of every country in the world except the United States.[2] Banks and other financial institutions provide capital in multiple forms, products, and derivatives. People at financial firms can be helpful, but they view "time is money," and they will expect you to know their industry's playing field and ground rules.

This chapter presents an overview of the financing industry and ways to raise capital. You'll learn about the various types of financing vehicles, including both traditional debt and equity financing, as well as newer ones such as crowdfunding. The chapter then lays out the various sources of capital available on both the debt and equity sides of the ledger. Since entrepreneurs have special needs, there is additional information for their raising capital.

Before we scrutinize the types and sources of capital available, let's start with a review of the bigger picture: money management and its strategic implications.

Money Management

In many ways, managing money is a tricky balancing game. All business entities need to balance incoming cash and outgoing expenses with a close eye on timing. Negative cash flow will eventually force a company into bankruptcy or to be sold at a distressed price. Early-stage companies—even if focused on growth rather than profits—need capital to cover production costs and pay for employees, offices, utilities, and other "overhead" expenses.

Companies in the process of trying to raise capital need to balance the amount of debt and equity. *Debt financing* is money borrowed to be repaid at a later date for a fee or interest. *Equity financing* is when capital is received in exchange for immediate or future ownership of the company. Within these broad two categories, there are several types of financing vehicles that address specific situations, company sizes, and stages of growth. (I'll describe these shortly.)

The way a company balances its debt and equity, known as *capital structure*, impacts its ability to attract new funds. Potential investors and lenders examine the balance sheet to assess the debt-to-equity ratio. This financial measure reveals the solvency of the company, meaning its ability to meet short- and longer-term obligations. A healthy company has both a sensible debt-to-equity ratio as well as significant liquidity, which is the sum of its cash plus its assets that are easily convertible to cash.[3]

Other factors also will play an important role when it comes to managing money, particularly for international businesses and entrepreneurs. These include the following:

Cost of capital is a critical measure since payback expense can be a burdensome hurdle. The "cost" of the capital you borrow through debt financing is mostly determined by the interest rate or percentage. Commercial lenders' rates are tied to the Federal Reserve bank rate, which is periodically adjusted based on economic conditions and monetary policy. The cost of capital from equity financing is more complicated, but basically it is the amount of money, or returned profits, demanded by your investors. Both lenders and investors look to minimize their risk and maximize their potential return. The riskier the deal, the more it will cost in interest rates and the more collateral you'll need to show the lender. You will also need to pay the money back sooner on a risky proposition.

A good strategy to lower the cost of capital is to reduce the perceived risk to potential investors and lenders. This is accomplished by presenting an attractive "win-win" opportunity, supported with a strong business plan and capable management team. You also should demonstrate that, in developing the plan, you've accounted for pessimistic, realistic, and optimistic scenarios of business growth and financial conditions.

Control refers to the amount of influence more than the business entity's management decisions you will maintain. The amount of ownership and control you are asked to relinquish in exchange for capital is an important consideration for business owners. Equity shares provide both value growth plus the opportunity to influence the use of capital. If an investor owns a large percentage of shares, they can become a director or, at least, have a voice in the board's decisions. Lenders also seek control or influence on board directors' decisions in order to reduce the risk of loan defaults.[4]

Timing for repaying debt and delivering investor returns needs to be closely watched when raising capital. Difficult-to-achieve obligations create stress on the management team. If the company takes on too much short-term debt, it could default on the loans and possibly go bankrupt. If it sells too much equity too soon, the owners can lose control of decision-making authority. Therefore, a good strategic approach is to raise capital, balanced between debt and equity, before the company actually needs it.

Banking relationships can help or hinder the ease and ability to raise capital. Without a U.S. credit history and established relationship, it can be difficult for foreign companies to secure loans and credit from U.S. banks. As a result, foreign parent companies often become the money lender to their U.S. subsidiaries to fund expansions. This can create a problem if the debt-to-equity ratio is too high, because the U.S. Internal Revenue Service will recharacterize all of the debt as equity when assessing taxes.[5]

Special Challenges for Entrepreneurs

Startup founders often struggle to raise capital. Without assets to use as collateral, banks hesitate to lend them money. Many great ideas never launch because entrepreneurs—foreign and U.S.-born alike—can't find sufficient funds to build products, hire talent, and scale the operation. Other startups grow too fast and run out of capital to support additional expenses.

Fortunately, the U.S. financial system offers many options (such as venture capital funding and private equity investors) and a large pool of eager investment money to lend to promising startups and scale-ups. Venture capital funding, for example, was at $330 billion for 2021, which was roughly double the amount in 2020.[6]

Nonetheless, entrepreneurs need to be strategic and savvy about how they raise funds. Done incorrectly, early rounds of funding can create complications for later, bigger deals. One Silicon Valley venture investor decided not to buy a technology company for $100 million, after learning that 4 percent of the company's stock was owned by 285 individuals who each invested less than $500 through an online crowdfunding platform. He didn't want to spend his time managing the constant emails from nonaccredited, unsophisticated investors asking how the company is doing. Does that mean you shouldn't consider crowdfunding as a way to find capital? Not necessarily. The point is you should seek advice from finance professions to make sure you're aware of any pitfalls before accepting a funding source.

Debt Financing

Every company uses some form of debt, even if it's just credit cards for small purchases. Americans call such business debt *leverage*, and they consider it a positive thing: Successful businesses are those that are able to borrow more money. Investment firms and individual investors rely on leverage, because it enables them to place bigger bets by borrowing against their existing holdings.

There are numerous types of debt vehicles, depending on the organization's size, stage of maturity, and riskiness of its business. In the next section, I'll tell you where to get loans and other debt vehicles. But first let's look at the most common types of debt capital instruments.

- **Debt securities** are bonds, notes, and debentures issued to raise capital. Bonds are obligations secured by an asset, such as an office building, owned by the borrowing organization. Debentures and notes are unsecured obligations issued for companies with strong business reputations. Debt securities are commonly issued through an underwriting process by one or more securities firms or banks that purchases and sells debt to investors.

- **Loans** are the most popular way businesses secure capital. Most are short-term loans from commercial banks that are paid back within 3 to 18 months. Short-term loans typically range from $2,500 to $250,000, and they can be secured in as little as two days. Banks also provide larger mid- and long-term loans that need to be repaid in one to five years, and they can range in size from $25,000 to $500,000.[7]
- **Business lines of credit** are the promise of cash to arrive when the company or individual needs it. Since there is no immediate outlay of cash, a company can secure a relatively larger line of credit than it could from a loan. Lines of credit are generally from $10,000 to more than $1 million. Armed with a strong business model and management team, a line of credit can be secured relatively fast and easily in the United States.
- **Property and equipment financing** is debt used to purchase a building, factory, or piece of equipment. In a sense, you never really own the item while you use it. The title or deed documenting ownership is held until all the payments are paid. The financing terms vary widely and are dependent on many factors, including the percentage of property or equipment you are financing and the supply and demand for the property or piece of equipment.
- **Invoice financing** is an advance of funds for sold products and services. Companies often have to wait 60 to 90 days to get paid after delivering an invoice or bill of sale. This is especially true when a third-party distributor or retailer is involved in the sale. With invoice financing,

companies can start to spend anywhere from 50 percent to 90 percent of the invoice amount. Of course, there is a fee or charge from the invoice financing company for being able to use the money.

- **Convertible securities** are bonds that give the owner the right to convert it into another security, such as common stock, from the same issuer. These financial instruments are similar to options because they can be used to purchase equity shares at an agreed price and time. For early-stage companies, convertible securities enable it to borrow money at a lower interest rate. Convertible securities are popular with angel investors and venture capital firms when doing deals with startup founders.

Where to Find Debt Financing

There are many sources for companies seeking capital, such as bonds, loans, and other debt vehicles. Here is an overview of the types of financial institutions and other players that provide debt capital:

- **Commercial banks** provide loans, mostly short- and mid-term, to businesses (as opposed to retail banks, which serve individuals). Commercial banks offer attractive interest rates and terms to companies with good credit rating and demonstrated ability to repay loans and provide collateral. Bankers tend to be conservative investors, so they seldom lend to risky ventures.
- **Commercial finance companies** lend money to a wide range of companies, including those deemed too risky by traditional banks. Commercial finance companies have more flexibility, since they are subject to fewer federal and state regulations. Interest rates are higher than from traditional banks, although they might provide lower rates if packaged with other services, such as accounts receivables and payroll management.[8]

- **Leasing companies** provide financing for equipment, furniture, and other business assets. Different than a loan, businesses pay the amount over time for the use of the asset. In some cases, the company must sign a service contract for the asset. Since the piece of equipment is considered collateral, the interest rate and terms can be attractive.
- **Suppliers** provide companies with needed raw materials, resources, and services under an agreement that the supplier will be paid at a later date. Usually, but not always, the payment will be made with an added fee. Since customers and the distribution channel can be slow to pay, this can be a valuable source of working capital.
- **Customers** can also be a source of capital. It's not unusual to receive payment in advance for some or all of a purchase. This up-front payment can fund the materials and labor needed to build a high-cost item for the customer. In some instances, a group of customers form a consortium to provide a bigger pool of financing.
- **Economic development organizations (EDOs)** provide loans and other incentives to attract businesses and jobs to their states, cities, and regions. These government-funded organizations actively compete for international and startup businesses. In addition to arranging loans with local banks, they provide tax credits, rebates, and exemptions; grants of money and forgivable loans; financing and aid for site development; and funding for job training and other startup costs. EDOs can also facilitate reduced rates and incentives from energy and other utility providers.[9]
- **Small Business Administration (SBA).** This branch of the federal government seeks to make "the American dream of business ownership a reality." The SBA guaranteed more than $28 billion loans in 2020 to small businesses, with 27 percent going to minority business owners.[10] In 2021 the SBA distributed more than $416 billion in emergency relief to small businesses, due to the pandemic.[11] International businesspeople and entrepreneurs are eligible. As the SBA states, financing is available

for businesses that are 51 percent owned and controlled by people who are not citizens of the United States provided that the people are lawfully in the United States.

Equity Financing

Equity financing is capital secured from investors in exchange for a share of ownership in the business. This equity provides a capital foundation for growth. There are both public exchanges and private markets for buying and selling equities. U.S. capital markets are especially attractive because they provide liquidity, which is the ease that securities can be converted into cash without affecting its market price. Here is an overview of the various equity vehicles:

- **Common stock** is an equity security that represents ownership of a portion of the corporation. It entitles the owner to a fraction of the enterprise's assets and profits. Common stockholders also receive the right to vote for directors and on company policies, usually at one vote per share. However, common stockholders are paid last on liquidations of company assets—only after creditors, bondholders, and preferred shareholders get paid.
- **Preferred stock** is similar to common stock, although preferred stockholders do not have voting rights. Instead, they are generally paid dividends—returns from company profits—before the common stockholders are paid. In some cases, investors of preferred stock receive a guaranteed fixed dividend, similar to a bond, during the years they hold the stock. There are other forms of preferred stock, too.
- **Warrants and options** provide holders the right to buy shares at a specific price within a specified period of time. A stock warrant is issued directly by a company. Stock options can be received from the company or purchased in a private transaction or public market. Early-stage companies often give employees stock options as

an incentive to either join or stay with the company. However, if the company's stock price never rises above the option price, the options don't have any value and are considered "under water."

- **Simple agreement for future equity (SAFE)** refers to an agreement that is often used by entrepreneurs to raise capital to fund the people and resources needed to support growth. The advantage of these simple agreements is that they can happen fast and with minimal legal fees. While they are somewhat similar to convertible securities, SAFEs do not have a maturity date.

Where to Find Equity Financing

There are many sources of equity capital for business entities. Here is an overview of the major sources:

- **Investment banks** formed after the Glass-Steagall Banking Act of 1993, which prohibited banks from purchasing, issuing, selling, or distributing debt and equity. Investment banks help companies raise capital by underwriting bonds, debentures, and stocks, including initial public offerings (IPOs). They also facilitate corporate mergers and acquisitions (M&A). (See the Alpina Foods case study at the end of this chapter, which tells the story of its acquisition efforts aided by an investment bank.)
- **Private equity firms** invest in private companies and publicly traded companies with the intention of taking them private. Typically, they create closed-end funds with investments from limited partners, including pension funds, university endowments, and wealthy individuals. Since PE firms are not publicly traded, they face fewer government regulations and documentation requirements. They supply loans, they purchase equity, and they engage in complex financing vehicles such as leverage buyouts (LBOs) and mezzanine debt.[12]

- **Venture capital (VC) firms** are the leading providers of equity and debt capital to early-stage companies. The United States has 2,889 active VC firms that invested $332 billion in 14,411 companies in 2021.[13] Venture capitalists are known to wait five to eight years to see a return on their investment, which occurs when a company grows enough for an IPO or when they are acquired by another firm. VCs pride themselves on providing valuable business advice, experience, and connections to nurture their portfolio companies. Usually they invest in stages, or rounds of financing, in return for additional shares based on agreed valuations.
- **Private investors** range from a few high–net worth individuals to family offices and investment clubs. Often wealthy, retired, or semiretired executives are willing to invest in a business they can help with their money, experience, and connections. Entrepreneurs commonly look to their family and friends for capital to start their venture. Moreover, most startup accelerator programs routinely introduce entrepreneurs to private investors and angel investors.
- **Angel investors** are similar to private investors, but these individuals tend to focus on the early stages of a company, sometimes when the business is merely an idea. Professional angels invest small sums with many startups with the hope a few of these small bets will pay off with huge returns. David S. Rose, founder of New York Angels, says these companies are like tiny plants, striving to become giant trees, so the first investments in them are called *seed investments*.[14]
- **Corporate investors** are another source of capital for small and emerging companies. Many large companies—including Amazon, Google, and Intel—make strategic investments in startups and scale-ups. Often these investments are to help them gain new capabilities and product ideas; sometimes such investments simply help grow their ecosystem. Amazon has a $200 billion venture fund

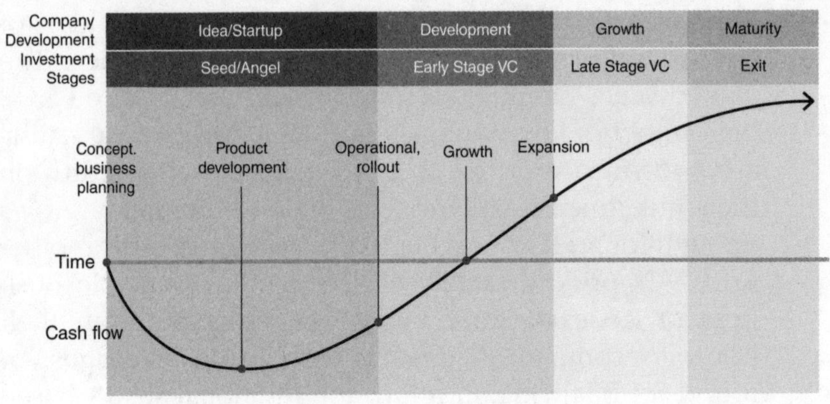

Figure 8.1 Venture capital and startup growth chart
Source: PitchBook Data, Inc. and NCVA Yearbook 2022

that invests in companies developing audio-recognition applications to support Amazon's Echo system.[15] The attractiveness of these investors is the likelihood of an exit through a merger or acquisition.

- **Crowdfunding** is a relatively new source for equity financing. With crowdfunding, small sums are invested by many people through online platforms. Historically, private markets were available only to institutions and the ultra-wealthy. The Jumpstart Our Business Startups (JOBS) Act of 2012 revised U.S. federal securities laws so crowdfunding could be used to offer and sell securities to the general public. SeedInvest, StartEngine, and Wefunder jumped in, offering vetted investment opportunities. Other crowdfunding platforms emerged to enable small investors to participate in larger deals. Republic has provided more than 600 companies with $700 million of investment capital between 2017 and 2022, including providing capital to the aerospace company SpaceX founded by Elon Musk.[16]

Joint Ventures

Another strategy for entering and scaling in U.S. markets is with a joint venture (JV). JVs are generally formed to share costs or secure needed capabilities, although sometimes they come with an infusion of capital as well. Another benefit is the acquisition of market knowledge, experience, and business connections. Typically, a new C corporation is formed with each side owning an agreed-on share of the entity. If you go this route, make sure to enlist a qualified lawyer to ensure your international company is able to continue its U.S. operation in the event of a change in circumstances or disputes between the parties.

International firms often enter into JVs with U.S. companies that can provide production capabilities. In other cases, JVs are formed with U.S. companies that provide sales, marketing, and distribution for their products. They find it faster, cheaper, and less risky than building their own U.S. sales organization. There are also JVs where international and U.S. companies jointly engage in research and development activities together.

Which Type and Source of Capital Should You Choose?

The decision whether to secure capital through debt or equity depends on how much is needed and how quickly, and how much ownership your company is willing to give up. The decision on what type of capital to seek has ramifications for the long-term health of the company and its prospects for raising more capital down the road. Just as with business strategy, every situation is different, so there is no easy answer.

The decision of where to get the capital is equally important. Will the financing entity be a good strategic partner who offers more than just money, such as business advice and experience? Will they share your objectives for long-term growth, or will they just be looking to get a quick return on their investment?

For early-stage and international companies, U.S. partners provide valuable connections to other resources and potential customers. Businesspeople often refer to these sources as *smart money*. Timing plays a major role in capital decisions. Ideally, you want to secure capital at a time when you can set the terms rather than being forced to borrow money at a high interest rate or sell equity. Then you'll be able to get an attractive deal or wait for a better time.

Research is crucially important. Dietmar Rieg of the German-American Chamber of Commerce calls this "doing your homework."[17] You'll get faster and better results by going to the right source for the capital you want. The U.S. financial system is huge and competitive, so firms specialize. The big financial services institutions have amassed lots of specialists. If your medical technology startup is looking for seed money to launch, then you'll do best to find angel investors who like to invest in your category.

My recommendation is to get the advice and attention of a smart finance person or group. Even if your international company has a financial genius onboard, it's still important to have someone who knows how to operate in the U.S. financial system. People in the industry will be impressed with your professionalism and openness to seek expert advice and talent.

In the next chapter, we'll look at understanding American culture and business practices. But first, let's look at the case study of a Colombian company that ran into capital financing problems.

Case Study: Alpina Foods (Colombia)

Alpina Productos Alimenticios Alpiecuador, S.A., is a dairy and food company based in Colombia. When Julián Jaramillo became chief executive officer in 2002, it had revenue of $211 million with 500 employees. When he retired in 2013, Alpina had grown to $935 million with 7,000 employees, mostly due to international expansion. But that level of success was not to last.

Here is Julián's story. After earning a master's degree in business and finance at University of Bogota, he worked for Banco de Crédito and then multinational corporations BASF and Kodak. He was smart and worldly, and later he attended executive programs at Northwestern University, Massachusetts Institute of Technology, University of California at Berkeley, New York University, and University of Pennsylvania.

Alpina decided to expand to the United States in 2007. At that time, the $6 billion U.S. yogurt market was growing 12–15 percent annually, and it was dominated by two French brands, Danone and Yoplait. Julián convinced the board of directors to explore the United States and its growing population of 30 million Hispanics. Internally, its U.S. initiative was called "El Sueño Americano"—The American Dream.[18]

Alpina created a U.S. subsidiary in 2009 and opened a corporate office in Miami, Florida. It planned to copy the company's own strategy already successfully used to expand to Ecuador, Peru, and Venezuela. It did this first by exporting products and then by acquiring local companies and building manufacturing plants in those countries. But then the New York Department of Sanitation started limiting dairy products from South America, because of food safety concerns. That's when Alpina accelerated its search for a U.S. production facility.

With the help of a U.S. investment bank, Alpina found an attractive midsize dairy company in Portland, Oregon. In addition to manufacturing facilities, it had a strong, regional brand and good relations with retailers in the Northwest. Alpina's board of directors rejected this acquisition because of its location. It believed Alpina should start on the East Coast where there were more people with South American roots.

(*continued*)

(*continued*)

Next the team found an under-utilized factory near Richmond, Virginia, for sale. Since Alpina would be buying the building and equipment, it would be a less-complicated deal. The board of directors rejected this idea, however, because they thought it would be better to have a more efficient, new factory. Instead, they wanted to pursue a particular strategy, known as a *green-field investment*, to build production and distribution operations from the ground up.

In 2011, Alpina built a new factory in Batavia, New York, which was near several dairy farms and only a five-hour drive to New York City. The local government incentivized them with a $767,096 tax reduction. The cost to buy the land and build the factory was $20 million, and over the next six years, Alpina was reported to have invested an additional $50 million to expand the plant.[19]

The U.S. Launch

Alpina knew it needed local talent for its entry into the competitive U.S. market. So it hired a consulting firm headed by Sergio Zyman, former chief marketing officer at Coca-Cola. Alpina also engaged Dr. Clotaire Rapaille, anthropologist and author of the bestselling book *The Culture Code*, for insights into American consumers. In addition, it hired Leo Burnett Advertising and Universal McCann to develop a multimedia campaign to support the launch.

The team decided to focus on women with a new brand, Alpina Restart, that combined fat-free yogurt with crunchy granola to the wide audience of women. As described by Carlos Ramirez, Alpina USA general manager: "Whether women are succeeding or slipping in their efforts, Alpina empowers them to 'Restart' with a tasty, better-for-you solution. We know that women are busy juggling their professional and family lives, so we made Restart perfectly convenient for wholesome, on-the-go nutrition."[20]

Alpina launched a campaign in NYC in 2011 with advertising, product sampling, store displays, and a social media program called "Wish for Women." The campaign helped Alpina grow from being available in 80 stores to more than 400 in six weeks. However, Alpina didn't account for the high cost of securing and maintaining distribution. Retailers charge fees to stock items in warehouses and stores (called *slotting fees*). A typical grocery chain with 1,000 stores charges approximately $40,000 to slot each item or stock-keeping unit (SKU). Since Restart came in four flavors, the cost to distribute the line in a single supermarket chain was $160,000. Additional costs were incurred for promotions, in-store displays, and retailers returning expired dairy products.

Even when displayed in stores, consumer sales for Restart were less than planned. When the marketing plan was developed, Chobani hadn't been considered a competitor. The thicker, less sweet, Greek yogurt brand quickly changed the tastes and buying habits of American consumers. Launched in 2007, Chobani skyrocketed to $460 million in sales and 10.3 percent market share by 2011.[21]

To generate revenue to cover its capital expenditures, therefore, Alpina started to manufacture products for other companies. This practice, known as *co-packing*, enabled it to keep the factory running at efficient levels. This worked for a while until Alpina lost its largest co-packing customer. Faced with high costs and little prospect to increase volume for its own brands without major funding, Alpina closed its U.S. manufacturing plant in late 2018. The factory was then sold to a regional dairy cooperative for $22.5 million.[22]

(*continued*)

(*continued*)

Today Alpina still has a Miami office, but its market presence is limited to stores that cater to Latin American consumers. In the mainstream market, according to Information Resources, Inc. (IRI)—a data analytics and market research company that tracks products sold in supermarkets; grocery, drug, and convenience stores; and other retail outlets—Alpina yogurts sold just $333,000 in 2016, $181,000 in 2017, and nothing after 2019.

Lessons from This Case Study

1. **Early decisions matter.** High costs and challenging debt terms present problems. It forces high goals and aggressive strategies to cover those costs and yield a return on the investment. Alpina's decision to build a factory resulted in an untenable financial decision.
2. **Investigate the cost of doing business.** Food and other U.S. markets have complex, multilayered sales and distribution systems. Each link in the chain has associated cost, which are best to know from the start. Alpina didn't anticipate the cost of securing and maintaining store presence, which led to the company's loss of profits.
3. **Expertly manage cash.** It takes an expert to balance incoming revenue with outgoing cost for capital and operations. One pitfall can lead to a cash crisis. Alpina relied on revenue from co-packing. When that revenue disappeared, it was unable to maintain positive cash flow.
4. **Competitive landscapes shift fast.** When Alpina planned its U.S. entry, it had looked at only the two major competitors. It totally missed Chobani, launched in 2007, that changed the entire dynamics in the yogurt business with both consumers and retailers.

Notes

1. "A Quote by Robert Herjavec," Goodreads, Accessed January 13, 2022. www.goodreads.com/quotes/6209807-cash-is-the-lifeblood-of-your-business-there-are-very
2. "Financial Services Industry Spotlight," SelectUSA, Accessed July 1, 2021, www.selectusa.gov/financial-services-industry-united-states
3. Andrew Sherman, *Raising Capital, Third Edition* (New York: AMACOM Books, 2012), pp. 4–6.
4. Ibid. p. 5.
5. Notion Insights, "Crossing the Atlantic," Notion Capital, 2017, p. 111.
6. "Q4 2021 PitchBook-NVCA Venture Monitor | PitchBook," Accessed May 4, 2022, pitchbook.com/news/reports/q4-2021-pitchbook-nvca-venture-monitor
7. Shepherd, Maddie, "Top Online Business Loan Options in 2022 and How to Apply," Accessed January 16, 2022, www.fundera.com/business-loans/guides/online-business-loan
8. Andrew Sherman, *Raising Capital, Third Edition* (New York: AMACOM Books, 2012), p. 8.
9. David Hickey and Jason Hickey, "Economic Development Incentives," SelectUSA, Select USA Investor Guide 2021, pp. 125–135.
10. Shannon Giles, "SBA Achieves Historic Small Business Lending for Fiscal Year 2020," U.S. Small Business Administration, October 28, 2020, www.sba.gov/article/2020/oct/28/sba-achieves-historic-small-business-lending-fiscal-year-2020
11. Jessica Merritt, "Small-Business Loans," U.S. News & World Report, January 3, 2022, money.usnews.com/loans/small-business-loans/best-small-business-loans#how-do-small-business-loans-work
12. Alicia Phaneuf, "Financial Services Industry Overview in 2022: Trends, Statistics & Analysis," Insider Intelligence, Accessed January 19, 2022, www.insiderintelligence.com/insights/financial-services-industry
13. "NCVA Yearbook 2022," National Venture Capital Association, Accessed May 5, 2022, www.nvca.org/research/nvca-yearbook/
14. David S. Rose, *Angel Investing* (Hoboken, NJ: John Wiley & Sons, Inc., 2014), p. 5.
15. "Amazon provides $200 million in venture capital funding – Alexa Fund Official Site," Amazon (Alexa), Accessed January 3, 2022, developer.amazon.com/en-US/alexa/alexa-startups/alexa-fund.html
16. "About," Republic website, Accessed February 12, 2022, republic.com/about
17. Conversation with Dietmar Rieg, president of German-American Chamber of Commerce, on March 25, 2021
18. Conversation with J. Jaramillo, former CEO of Alpina, on May 4, 2021

19. Howard Owens, "Buyers Lining Up for Alpina Plant at Bargain Price Compared to $70 Million Invested," The Batavian, January 24, 2019, www.thebatavian.com/howard-b-owens/buyers-lining-up-for-alpina-plant-at-bargain-price-compared-to-70-million-invested
20. "We Talk To, Not At, Women," Dairy Foods, October 14, 2011, www.dairyfoods.com/articles/86476-we-talk-to-not-at-women?v=preview
21. Mamta Badkar, "Trendy Greek Yogurt Chobani is Officially the Top Selling Brand in America, Insider, Inc., Oct. 8, 2011, www.businessinsider.com/americas-favorite-yogurt-2011-10
22. James Fink, "Upstate Niagara Buys Alpina Foods Plant in Batavia," The Business Journals, April 17, 2019, www.bizjournals.com/buffalo/news/2019/04/17/upstate-niagara-buys-alpina-foods-plant.html

9

Understanding Americans

"I've been living and working in the United States for over 20 years, and I still don't understand Americans," a French-born executive of a global enterprise told me recently. His comment echoed the findings in my survey of more than 100 international executives and entrepreneurs, who said they needed to better understand American customs, culture, and ways of doing business.

In subsequent interviews, many of those businesspeople said they most worried about making cultural missteps that would impede their success, and they said American consumers and businesspeople were difficult to understand. Some found Americans overly tough and critical, and others found them soft and insincere. A Dutch executive asked why Americans are so enthusiastic and friendly all the time. He couldn't understand why Americans gush about routine meetings being "great" and "exciting." To him it sounded phony and insincere: "Did the American just win the lottery?" he said, exasperated. He was also confused why U.S. businesspeople want to jump right into talking about business after quick introductions. In Europe, he explained, the "warm up" conversation is at least twice as long as it is here.

Several expats said they experienced "culture shock" shortly after moving to the United States. The people they met were very different and more complicated than the actors on American movies and television shows. Even though many had studied English in school, these expats soon discovered they didn't fully understand American English. A German said she lacked "Sprachgefühl," which translates to understanding the essential character of a language and having an intuitive feel for the idioms. A Korean woman told of studying the TV series *Friends* to learn American idioms and expressions but still had trouble making actual American friends after moving here. Other people complained about the overwhelming number of books, articles, and stories about American culture, which only seemed to obscure the real issues rather than illuminate them.

To clarify the confusion around culture, I will explain in this chapter the core differences and underlying drivers of Americans' mindset and behaviors. Specifically, I will present several well-respected research findings and theoretical models on national cultures. The chapter also includes a closer look at doing business in the United States, along with some practical recommendations on communicating and working with Americans. Armed with these frameworks and guidance, you will be equipped to better understand American norms in social and business settings.

But first, let's set the stage by defining culture and why each society has a somewhat different one.

What Is Culture?

Anthropologists define culture as the way groups of people think, feel, and act. Some say culture is the emotional preferences that members in a society have in common for both everyday and momentous decisions. These preferences are shaped by the group's shared values on what's right and wrong, what's proper and improper, and what's normal and abnormal. Culture can be seen in the values, rituals, heroes, and symbols in a society.

- **Values.** The principles and ideals held by most people in the society.
- **Rituals.** The collective activities, including ceremonies, and ways people interact.

- **Heroes.** People admired by the group, including leaders and storybook characters.
- **Symbols.** Meaningful images, styles, and badges of status shared by the group.

Note that these cultural elements are shared by most, but not all, members of a society. For example, most—but not all—Americans believe in the values of freedom and independence, and they cherish symbols such as the Statue of Liberty and the bald eagle. They are cultural norms, which social scientists calculate as the average or median of the total group. Visually, it's the top of the bell curve between two descending curves.

Another way to think about cultural norms is that individuals are merely informed by the preferences shared by the group. The preeminent cross-cultural researcher Geert Hofstede presented this concept in a three-leveled pyramid, with culture sandwiched between human nature and individual personality. Human nature describes the basic physical and psychological functions inherent to all people. Every person is born with the inherited capacity to feel anger, joy, fear, love, and shame. What one *does* with those feelings is modified by culture. Individual

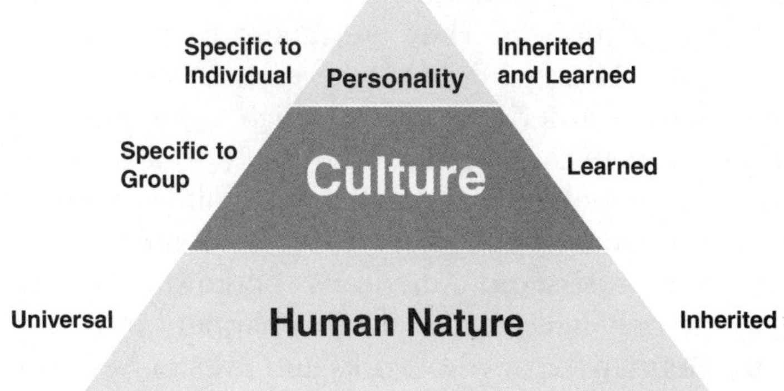

Figure 9.1 Culture triangle
Source: Hofstede, *Cultures and Organizations*, 2010

personalities are influenced by the cultural attitudes and behaviors experienced in their upbringing.[1]

One of my graduate students, who was from Spain, described the phenomenon of culture like this: "People want to feel unique, but not alone. Culture permits entry to that safe space." Her recognition of the importance and value of common cultural ties might be due to living alone for the first time in a new country, which was made even more difficult during the COVID lockdown period.

How Do Cultures Form?

Culture is learned at an early age, especially from birth to six years of age, according to Hofstede and other cultural psychologists. Generally, people think and act in ways they learned from parents, teachers, siblings, and friends. We observe and imitate the behaviors and attitudes of the people we encounter at a young age. These cultural preferences get passed down to our children and their children. National and regional cultures developed because people tended to stay in the communities of their birth.

Let's go back to the comment by the Dutch executive about Americans being overly enthusiastic and disingenuous. Children in the United States are trained in schools and social settings to be friendly and upbeat. They are taught to say "Hello," "Hi," "Howdy," and "How ya doin'?" to everyone they meet. It's an ingrained part of American culture, which to people from other countries often feels superficially friendly. But to Americans, the friendly greeting is a ritual that signifies every human deserves to be acknowledged and feel welcomed.

To better understand Americans' optimism and "can do" attitude, you only need to look at what happens in U.S. schools. Irene is a German expat who works and lives in New York City. She observed how American culture was "taught" in her five-year-old child's public school. On Earth Day the teacher asked the students how they could help save the planet. The discussion was positive, optimistic, and proactive. The students offered ideas such as, "I could switch off the light when I leave the room," and "I could stop using plastic straws." Irene told me this was starkly different from her experience in German schools, which focused on rules and "what *not* to do." She said that German schoolchildren might have suggested something very different in tone—for example, "Don't pollute the sky" or "Don't throw things in the ocean."

One American Culture?

As explained in Chapter 6, the United States is not one homogenous country. It is huge in size and diverse in climates, resources, and ethnicities. You might wonder, then: Is it possible and useful to identify a single American culture?

The answer is "yes," but the culture should be viewed as just a starting point for digging deeper to fully understand the Americans you encounter. The task starts by examining the cultural norms existing across the United States and then looking for variations among the many subcultures defined by regions, communities, and ethnic groups. (See the case study at the end of this chapter, which recounts the plight of a U.K. company, Tesco, that failed to understand American culture when attempting to launch grocery stores into U.S. markets.)

Here's a juicy metaphor: the all-American hamburger—beloved by people across our nation. Americans take pride in their burgers, and they order them by the billions in fast-food restaurants and roadside diners. (Never mind that the food was originally conceived in Hamburg, Germany!) While a national treasure, the hamburger appears in several variations, depending on the region and subgroup. Northeasterners prefer burgers topped with ketchup and mustard. West Coasters and Midwesterners are strictly ketchup only. Mexican-Americans like burgers covered with chili salsa. Indian-Americans cook burgers with ginger, garlic, coriander, and garam masala powder and serve them with a spiced mayonnaise sauce.

The preparation of the burger is a distinctly American ritual, too. Memorial Day holiday in late May marks the start of the summer season. Burgers take center stage, typically on the outdoor BBQ grill of an aproned chef surrounded by family members. Burgers enter American diets early in life. McDonald's restaurants, with its golden arches and gleaming counters, are practically a rite of passage for American children, many of whom get their first Happy Meal® as toddlers.

Using Frameworks to Compare National Cultures

National cultures are relative. Therefore, it is useful to compare cultural norms in the United States to those in your home country. For example, people from time-flexible France, Brazil, and India view Americans as being perhaps overly punctual and strict about keeping deadlines and schedules. People from Germany, Switzerland, and Japan would say Americans are very loose about time.

Since there are so many cultural differences between people of various nations, it is helpful to use a framework to compare cultures and uncover the underlying reasons why societies think and behave the way they do. Frameworks provide a lens to observe cultural norms in an objective way—although I admit that some cultural norms, such as Americans' preference for weak and watery coffee, just can't be explained objectively or otherwise.

The frameworks presented in this chapter were developed by social scientists based on analysis of large-scale research data. The first cross-cultural model, which many consider definitive, was developed by Geert Hofstede in the 1970s. As a consultant to the global computer company IBM, he had access to more than 100,000 IBM employees in more than 60 countries who were similar in education, income, and other attributes. In researchers' terms, this database eliminated all variables except their country of origin. Subsequently, Hofstede's research was validated over four decades and expanded to compare cultural differences in approximately 100 countries.[2]

Hofstede discovered that people in different nations differ in just a few fundamental ways. He argued these cultural dimensions were tied to the way societies dealt with basic problems they encountered, for example, how the society handled inequality and how it reacted to the unknown. Because nations existed separately for centuries, each developed a unique set of cultural norms that were taught and reinforced in homes, schools, and playgrounds. Hofstede identified this "software of the mind" as the collective programming that distinguishes one group from another.[3]

Later Hofstede was questioned about whether it is possible to have national cultures, since multiple subgroups exist in every nation. He studied the research data to confirm that subgroups were more similar with other subgroups in their nation than with people in other nations. Research published in *Psychological Science* in 2020 confirmed that the United States is more culturally homogeneous than many other countries.[4]

Hofstede's groundbreaking work led to the creation of a data-driven model/framework across five cultural dimensions. The framework tracks each cultural dimension along a linear range between two extreme positions and produces a score for each country—from zero to 100—on each dimension. Below I'll describe each of the five dimensions: power distance, individualism versus collectivism, achievement orientation, uncertainty avoidance, and long-term versus short-term orientation. I will also describe a sixth dimension—indulgence versus restraint—which was added later, in 2010, by Hofstede's son, Gert Jan, and Dr. Michael Minkov in the third edition of *Cultures and Organizations*.

Power Distance. Power distance is the degree to which the less powerful members of a society accept and expect that power is distributed unequally. It measures how much a group listens to authority and obeys rules and regulations. Another way to describe power distance is the level of egalitarianism, which is the belief that all people are equal and deserve equal rights and opportunities.

In high power distance societies, there is a deference to authority and rules. Children are taught to obey and not challenge their parents, teachers, and elders. These nations, which include China, Mexico, and Russia, typically have centralized, hierarchical institutions. Decisions are made at the top, and workers expect to be told what to do. Bosses keep a distance from subordinates, often in chauffeured cars or secluded offices. Note that a full 85 percent of the world lives in high power distance societies.[5]

Nations with low power distance, such as the United States, Denmark, and Israel, are more egalitarian than others. Children are taught that their ideas and opinions are important. People can vote and have a say in how the country is run. Business organizations are typically decentralized and nonhierarchical, and workers aren't afraid to question authority. Leaders regularly interact with people at all levels of the organization.

In the United States, for example, companies generally have an "open door" policy, where workers are able to discuss issues and problems with their boss. These egalitarian values are rooted in the country's founding declaration that "all men are created equal." However, there are notable regional differences with regard to this dimension. Martin Karaffa is an associate partner at Hofstede Insights, a firm whose mission is to curate and expand the commercial application of Hofstede's cultural analytics. He points out that egalitarianism is strongest in Middle America. Coastal cities attract those who aspire, literally, to be close to the corridors of power. Hierarchical industries, such as Hollywood, Wall Street, Madison Avenue, and the venture capital circles of Silicon Valley, tend to attract individuals who accept higher power distance.

Individualism vs. Collectivism. Societies differ in how people think and act with regard to their responsibility to the collective group. People in individualistic societies are wired to take care of themselves and their immediate families first. They have a strong "I" orientation. They tend to make decisions by themselves. They believe speaking their minds is healthy, and they don't mind "rocking the boat."

People in collectivistic societies are wired to think of themselves within the context of a wider group. They have a strong "we" orientation, and they expect members of their ingroup to look after them. They make decisions as a group and enjoy collaborating with others. They tend to avoid confrontation and maintain harmony within the group rather than speak their mind.

The United States has the highest score for individualism than any nation. This value goes to the root of the country founded on the ideals of liberty and freedom, where children are encouraged to pursue their own dreams and wishes.

Individualism is one reason the United States seems polarized. Americans believe in expressing their thoughts and views. They band together in little tribes with like-minded, like-interested people and soon grow into a bigger group of individuals. Still, it's "I," but "I" includes more than one individual. Republicans and Democrats. Liberals and conservatives. Boston Red Sox baseball fans and New York Yankees fans.

Achievement Orientation. This dimension measures the importance to a country's citizens for personal achievement, material success, and status. It's the degree that people value winning and competition versus harmony and cooperation. A management consultant described this dimension as "rough versus tender" business cultures.

People in achievement-oriented societies believe competition is good, and winners deserve material rewards and higher status. Assertiveness is not only acceptable but admired. Children are taught that winning in sports, school, and life is paramount. Businesspeople spend more time in the office than at home. Many avoid going on vacations, afraid that they might fall behind their co-workers.

At the other end of the spectrum are societal-oriented nations, whose citizens largely prefer harmony and cooperation (over competition). There is an emphasis on caring for the weak rather than rewarding the strong. Quality of life is more important in these societies than climbing up the corporate ladder. In business and other institutions, decisions are made by consensus rather than by individual leaders. Vacations and time spent with family is considered necessary and sacrosanct. The Scandinavian countries are the most societal-orientated nations. Modesty and humbleness are valued, which the Swedes call "Jantelagen."

The United States is relatively high in achievement orientation. (Notably, American men score 20 percent higher than women on this dimension.) The nation is obsessed with the lives of winners in sports, entertainment, politics, and business. Displays of success in the form of luxury—"bling"—are admired and envied by most of the population. This achievement orientation is seen most readily in the business world. A top story on U.S. nightly news programs is always the Dow Jones Industrial Average. U.S. business leaders—such as Bill Gates, Warren Buffet, Steve Jobs, and Meg Whitman—are revered for their wealth and winning strategies. In fact, many businesspeople capitalize on their reputations to run for political office.

"Whether it's personal fulfillment, social inclusion, or respectability," said Steven Vallas, a Northeastern University sociology professor, "work is the single most important way of proving your worth as a person" in the United States.[6]

Uncertainty Avoidance. Uncertainty avoidance measures the degree to which a nation's people feel comfortable with ambiguity. It reflects how the society deals with an unknown future. In high uncertainty avoidance societies, people see uncertainty as a threat that causes stress and anxiety. New ideas are not welcome, and there is a comfort in following rules and routines. For example, the Spanish have a saying, "*Más vale malo concido que malo por conocer*," that translates to, "It's better to stick with the bad that is known rather than look for something better that is unknown."

In low uncertainty avoidance societies, uncertainty is considered normal and expected. It doesn't cause extreme stress or anxiety, and it can energize people and spur creativity. People are relatively tolerant of deviant ideas, and they have no problem changing jobs. In general, these people tend to dislike rules and regulations. People in the United States score relatively low in uncertainty avoidance, and generally, Americans are fairly comfortable with the unknown. They are open to trying new ideas and new approaches. This often stimulates people and organizations to be prepared for anything that might happen. U.S. investors embrace risk and are comfortable making big bets on ventures that might produce enormous returns. Americans are encouraged to "Go with the flow."

Long-Term vs. Short-Term Orientation. This dimension measures the degree to which a society focuses on immediate versus future events and goals. This includes how it chooses to maintain and continue the traditions and ideas of the past to solve current challenges.

Long-term-oriented societies focus on the future. People work toward future goals with sustained effort and perseverance, believing that the most important events have yet to occur. These societies are pragmatic, with people willing to save and invest in the future. Traditions are considered to be flexible and adaptable.

Short-term-oriented societies focus on immediate events and issues. People look to history and traditions for guidance because they think the most important events have occurred in the past. These people are concerned about social obligations and levels of status. Consumption and spending on today's problems takes precedence over investments for the future.

People in the United States are relatively short-term focused. Conversations are often about what's current and happening now. Americans like results and things to happen quickly. They are task-driven, often focused on checklists and having schedules. A visitor from the United States I know who traveled to Uganda was told by their host, "You Americans all have watches, but you have no time."

Martin Karaffa at Hofstede Insights compared long-term- and short-term-oriented countries with regard to car purchase with cash or credit. His analysis combined their national culture data with others' data on car purchases from 2013–2015. Their findings? In China and Germany, both long-term oriented, only 25 percent and 23 percent, respectfully, of cars were financed, while most were paid for in full at the time of purchase. In the short-term-oriented United States, on the other hand, 84 percent of cars were financed.

Indulgence vs. Restraint. This dimension measures the degree to which a society allows the gratification of personal needs and desires. People from more indulgent cultures will hesitate only minimally when there's an opportunity for self-gratification. On the opposite pole of this dimension, the society places a high value on thrift and restraint from impulsive wants. It's a value that is taught and reinforced by parents, teachers, and role models, and the behavior is portrayed either positively or negatively in the local media.

In high indulgent societies, people believe they have the freedom to live life as they please. It's important to engage in fun activities and have friends. In surveys, people in indulgent societies feel happier, healthier, and more in control of their lives than people do in restraint societies. In those cultures, which tend to restrain or control people's personal lives, for example, there is less emphasis on leisure time and having fun. Rules and regulations are important. People feel that if they indulge in activities for themselves and their families, they will be ostracized. According to Hofstede research, China and Russia score high on the restraint dimension.

Not surprisingly, the United States is tops on the indulgence dimension, along with Canada, Mexico, and the Scandinavian countries. Americans strive to live a full, rich life for themselves and their families. Americans play as hard as they work, rarely passing up an opportunity for spontaneous pleasure. And while Americans love to win, they also want others to be happy. Thus, they look for "win-win" situations, where both sides of the negotiating table can feel satisfied with the outcome. Then it is time to celebrate with drinks, food, and other indulgences.

Communication, American-Style

Americans are known to talk in a blunt and straightforward way. They "tell it like it is" and admire people who are open and honest. This communication style can be seen in American movies, television, and boardrooms. Parents and schools teach children the virtues of honesty and "speaking your mind." They hear stories about "Honest Abe" Lincoln and about George Washington confessing to cutting down his father's cherry tree.

Americans are taught to deliver any speech or talk according to the following formula: 1) tell the audience what you are going to say, 2) say it, and 3) tell them what you just said. Business proposals and presentations often start with a short executive summary and end with a conclusion and detailed next steps. The goal is for there to be no room for confusion or not getting the message.

To understand why Americans communicate this way, we need to examine the underlying reasons. The American anthropologist Robert T. Hall developed a theoretical framework in the 1960s to help people avoid the common error of "ignorance of the secret and hidden language of foreign cultures." He saw how people in Japan and other Asian cultures, for example, who shared a context of similar experiences, emotional triggers, and environment were able to communicate effectively without always having to use words. This unspoken language is what the Japanese call "listening to the air." Hall categorized groups on a scale between two opposite poles with regard to the context of the communication event. Then he scored nations between the axis of high-context and low-context cultures.

In high-context cultures, the society or group of people have had similar upbringing, family structures, educations, and other life experiences. They share common historical and cultural references. They don't have to rely just on spoken language to communicate, because they can infer meaning through connections about time, space, material things, friendships, and previous agreements.[7]

The United States is the lowest-context culture of any major country. With its population originating from so many diverse backgrounds and places, few citizens have had the same experiences, and there are few opportunities to share thoughts and ideas through words that have a secret meaning between friends. Plus, the country doesn't have a long history of existence. Therefore, the United States emphasizes the importance of clearly articulated language that won't be misunderstood. This style is evident both in the way people in the United States speak and in their desire to have things "spelled out" in writing.

Building on that work by Robert T. Hall as well as Hofstede's studies, Erin Meyer of INSEAD developed a useful model described in the popular 2014 book *The Culture Map: Breaking Through the Invisible Boundaries of Global Business*. Her theoretical model compares national cultures along eight dimensions, including how each communicates, builds trust, gives feedback, and makes decisions. Its goal is to help businesspeople to avoid missteps when entering foreign markets and communities. An online tool based on the model is available at erinmeyer.com/tools/. For a nominal cost it enables you to compare more than 60 countries along the eight dimensions.

American Business Culture

Luckily, you don't have to understand every aspect of American culture to do business in U.S. markets. You only have to be a good observer and be a fast learner, because we Americans are mostly transparent about our thinking and rituals. For example, generally in a business setting Americans will greet you with a warm handshake, and in more informal settings like dinner in someone's home, your hosts might even offer a hug at the beginning or end of the evening. Just take your cues from your American host or business colleague and reciprocate what they do whenever possible.

Generally, you can expect to see American values reflected in business organizations and operations. Gary Althen describes that phenomenon in his 2011 book *American Ways: A Cultural Guide to the United States of America*. His insights are based on more than 30 years at the University of Iowa advising foreign students how to navigate America's diverse and changing culture. The book points out many aspects of doing business in the United States, which I describe here along with a few of my own recommendations.

The "American work ethic" is real. While people in the United States often seem relaxed and easygoing, Americans generally work hard. The average American works 44 hours per week, or 8.8 hours per day.[8] In finance, law, technology, and other demanding fields, people are expected to work more than 60 hours per week. Children are taught at home and at school that hard work and diligence are morally good and will be rewarded with success. America's individualistic values reinforce the belief that every person can succeed with hard work. Our citizens love "rags to riches" stories about hardworking people who rose from humble beginnings to become winners in business, sports, and entertainment.

Punctuality and efficiency are key. Americans don't like to waste time. They like to get as many things done as quickly as possible in order to accomplish even more tasks. Children are taught the virtues of speed as "the early bird catches the worm." Later, they are taught in business schools about first-mover advantage. Therefore, promptness and schedules are important. Americans want meetings to start and end on time. There should be an agenda set and followed so that no one's time is wasted.

Relationships are secondary. Since Americans like to "get down to business" quickly, they place little importance on establishing a relationship. One European executive told me he arrived at a meeting in New York, was asked briefly how his trip was, and then the meeting began within minutes. Americans only need to feel they can trust you to deliver your end of the bargain. Therefore, don't feel insulted if your hosts don't express interest in you or your family. It's better to come to the business table with a good reputation and a warm introduction from a trusted source. Eventually, over the course of doing business, you might indeed build a more personal relationship with

American colleagues. But generally, you'll succeed simply if you and your U.S. counterpart enjoy a congenial working relationship.

Decisions are data driven. More and more Americans businesspeople look for "hard data" when making important decisions and sizable purchases. They rely on financial and market data, often from quantitative research, to analyze a business opportunity and associated risks. Certainly, the increased access to digital data has escalated the focus on evidence-based decision-making. Even creative industries are being driven by Big Data. Before Netflix invested $100 million in the *House of Cards* series, it analyzed viewership data from its more than 50 million subscribers to calculate its return on investment. Still, it is important to understand the underlying factors of the numbers. As you'll read in the case study on Tesco at the end of this chapter, trouble ensues when research data isn't appropriately analyzed.

Importance of written words. U.S. business puts more trust in documents than discussions. Agreements aren't final until a written contract is fully executed with signatures from all parties. In most cases, the particulars in written contracts override any verbal agreements. Even words in emails and social media carry more weight than verbal ones in legal suits. Often U.S. businesspeople will craft a memorandum of understanding (MOU) to outline a deal so parties can move forward while lawyers create formal contracts. In my consulting practice, I regularly document any agreements and information discussed. It both clarifies the communication and provides a helpful reference for future questions.

Know who has the authority. Another recommendation for doing business in the United States is to find out who at the organization will make the ultimate decision—even if the person you are negotiating with says, "So, do we have a deal?" Don't assume that person has the authority to finalize the deal. Most enterprises have strict rules and penalties for people making deals without the approval of their boss. For example, when I was vice president at Pitney Bowes, I was allowed to approve purchase orders up to $100,000. After that amount, I needed to get approval from the company president.

Now I'll conclude this chapter in good-old, American low-context communication style, by telling you what I just told you. To summarize, understanding Americans and doing business in the United States can be tricky. It requires careful investigation and research to uncover the cultural components and market dynamics. Even then, it requires curiosity and openness to finding the truth.

In the next chapter, we'll focus on building teams and navigating the U.S. visa and immigration system. But first, here is a case study about a company that didn't appreciate the cultural differences between the United Kingdom and the United States.

Case Study: Tesco (U.K.)

This is the story of a U.K. grocery company that went through the motions of research but never truly listened to those findings to understand the American market.

In 2006, Tesco was the largest supermarket chain in the United Kingdom, with annual sales of $70 billion. CEO Terry Leahy believed its technology prowess would spell success in U.S. market. It was the first European retailer to invest heavily in data science to analyze customer purchases and test variables of price, promotion, and store design.

After researching the U.S. market, Tesco determined its small grocery store concept, popular in United Kingdom, would fill the gap between large supermarkets and convenience stores such as 7-Eleven. It thought the British style of prepackaged produce and prepared foods would appeal to Americans' "on-the-go" lifestyle. It also felt middle-income families were underserved, as there was an abundance of supermarkets in wealthier U.S. neighborhoods.

(*continued*)

(*continued*)

Tesco opened six stores under the Fresh & Easy name in Southern California in November 2007, and within a year opened 150 across California, Arizona, and Nevada. The stores were about a third of the size of the average U.S. supermarket's 47,500 square feet, and each sold 4,000 items compared to 28,000 items in U.S. stores. Most were packaged, including fruits and vegetables wrapped in plastic. In the United Kingdom, Tesco's small grocery stores were located near train and subway stations, so in the United States they placed Fresh & Easy stores within walking distance of business and residential areas.

From the beginning, however, Fresh & Easy stores didn't meet sales projections. Average weekly sales were $50,000 to $60,000, which were 75 percent below the $200,000 target.[9]

What Went Wrong?

Basically, Tesco completely underestimated and misjudged the U.S. market. With $700 billion in annual sales, the U.S. grocery industry is the richest in the world. Most items are bought in the 38,300 supermarkets and even larger superstores.[10] The U.S. market has attracted numerous international companies. For example, Ahold Delhaize, headquartered in the Netherlands, is the fifth-largest player in the U.S. market, with sales of more than $44 billion from 1,973 supermarkets. It entered the market by buying Food Lion, Hannaford, and Stop & Shop supermarket chains.

Patrick Spear, CEO of Global Market Development Center (GMDC), a 50-year-old U.S. retail trade association, describes the U.S. grocery industry as brutally competitive. Profit margins are razor-thin and operating costs are high, so supermarkets need ample sales to break even.

U.S. customers are demanding, and they have a lot of choices of where to shop. The industry is highly regulated and under the close scrutiny of the Food & Drug Administration and the Department of Safety.

Patrick told me that Tesco made a lot of wrong decisions about the U.S. market. First, they picked the wrong locations. Southern California and Arizona were "two of the most over-stored markets in the country" with Walmart, Costco, and strong regional chains. Because of the heat and lack of public transportation in those markets, people drive rather than walk. The decision to wrap produce in plastic wasn't right for U.S. consumers. Americans like to inspect their lettuce, tomatoes, and other items to select the best of the bin. What's more, U.S. family sizes vary widely, so Tesco's one-sized package didn't meet all their needs.

Kevin Coupe, "Content Guy" for the retail industry blog MorningNewsBeat.com, attributes Tesco's failure to arrogance and hubris. They sent a team of people to study the U.S. market for nearly a year, including extensive data analysis and consumer interviews. However, they really didn't pay attention to or act on their findings. Instead, they tried to teach Americans to shop the British way, as opposed to adopting to the marketplace.

Kevin remembers visiting several Fresh & Easy stores in Scottsdale, Arizona—one in a predominantly white neighborhood and the other in a Hispanic neighborhood. Both stores had exactly the same English language magazines at the checkout counters. He wondered, "Wouldn't you want to have an offering that's tailored to the local community as opposed to a cookie-cutter approach?"

Lastly, timing didn't help Tesco. Their expansion of stores in 2008 and 2009 coincided with Great Recession. Unemployment rose, and families cut back on spending, even on food and household items.

(*continued*)

In the end, Tesco closed 12 stores in January 2012. Within a year it sold the remaining stores and exited the U.S. market at a reported loss of more than $1 billion.

Lessons from This Case Study

1. **Don't assume that success in your home country will translate here.** Tesco falsely assumed that its British concepts would work in U.S. markets. The case demonstrates the dangers of not appreciating the cultural differences in different nations.
2. **Be sure you understand U.S. markets and consumers.** Although Tesco conducted market research, they either did it badly or failed to pay close attention to the findings. The case demonstrates the difficulty of relying on market studies and data analytics from afar.
3. **Be flexible and adaptable.** Tesco never adjusted their stores and go-to-market strategies after early indications of problems. They should have adapted to the market dynamics in the Southwest and California regions, rather than stick to their original plans.
4. **Choose the locations carefully.** Tesco selected the wrong markets to enter. Every region, state, city, and neighborhood in the United States has different dynamics. It's important to select an initial location to demonstrate success before expanding to other markets.

Notes

1. Geert Hofstede, et al., *Cultures and Organizations: Software of the Mind*, 3rd Edition (New York: McGraw-Hill, 2010), pp. 4–13.
2. "Geert Hofstede's: The Dimension Paradigm," Hofstede Insights, Accessed April 19, 2022, hi.hofstede-insights.com/models
3. Geert Hofstede, et al., *Cultures and Organizations: Software of the Mind*, 3rd Edition (New York: McGraw-Hill, 2010), p. 6.

4. Michael Muthukrishna, et al., “Beyond Western, Educated, Industrial, Rich, and Democratic (WEIRD) Psychology: Measuring and Mapping Scales of Cultural and Psychological Distance,” *Psychological Science* 2020, Vol 31, p. 678–701
5. Lisa DeWaard, “The Dread Micromanagement,” Hofstede Insights, May 4, 2021, www.linkedin.com/pulse/dread-micromanagement-lisa-dewaard/?trackingId=BR69pC23pzr66%2FN7r7dKsw%3D%3D
6. Gil Malinsky, “‘Work is the single most important way of proving your worth’ in the U.S., professor says — and it’s making Americans miserable’” Grow from Acorns, February 10, 2021, grow.acorns.com/how-americans-relationship-with-work-affects-well-being
7. Edward T. Hall, “The SILENT LANGUAGE in Overseas Business,” *Harvard Business Review*, May 1960, pp. 87–96.
8. Marguerite Ward, “A brief history of the 8-hour workday, which changed how Americans Work,” CNBC Make It, May 3, 2017, www.cnbc.com/2017/05/03/how-the-8-hour-workday-changed-how-americans-work.html
9. John A. Quelch, “Case Study: Tesco PLC: Fresh & Easy in the United States,” Harvard Business School Publishing, November 5, 2010.
10. Progressive Grocer, “Number of supermarket stores in the United States from 2013 to 2018, by operator,” Chart, April 1, 2019, Statista, Accessed April 17, 2022, www-statista-com/statistics/240920/number-of-us-supermarket-stores-by-operator

10

Building Teams and Navigating Visas

Recruiting, interviewing, hiring, and managing a workforce may be the most challenging aspect of doing business in the United States. And yet, as Larry Bossidy, former chairman of Honeywell International, says, "I am convinced that nothing we do is more important than hiring and developing people. At the end of the day, you bet on people, not strategies."[1]

To be sure, if you hope to successfully enter and scale in U.S. markets, you'll need smart, capable, and dedicated people. People with the necessary skills and know-how to get the job done. People who can effectively manage teams and projects. People who are culturally a "good fit" with your organization's corporate culture and values. And, finally, people who you can afford to hire within your budget.

In the previous chapter, we explored how American culture is complex and unique, including the attitudes and behaviors around work. In addition, there are many legal differences from other countries, which is further complicated by the 50 states having different laws and regulations. For example, 30 U.S. states have laws that require a higher minimum wage than the federal rate, 15 have equal rates, and five states have no minimum wage legal requirements.[2]

This chapter provides a high-level overview of the U.S. employment landscape and business practices. It gives special attention to the early steps involved in recruiting and hiring employees, including the benefits that companies are expected to provide employees. Since you'll probably want workers from your home country—which might include you if you're a foreign national—there is an overview of the complicated U.S. visa and immigration system. In most cases, you'll need to consult with a U.S.-based attorney, but this chapter will help you prepare for that discussion.

Finally, the chapter ends with a case study on a European couple who successfully navigated the U.S. visa system on their way to start, scale, and sell a 200-person company providing pet insurance. Before embarking on that, let's examine U.S. employment practices.

Recruiting Your Team

The best hires are people who align well with the needs, culture, and vision of the organization. Therefore, start by looking inward. What talents and skills are most needed? Are there gaps in knowledge and experience to fill? What cultural values and attitudes do your best employees demonstrate? How much can you afford to pay each new hire?

Then get the word out. Start with current employees and their friends and families. If you don't know anyone in the United States, reach out to people on LinkedIn, Facebook, and other networking sites. Chambers of commerce, both from your home country and from the city where your company operates, can help you connect with potential employees. Be enthusiastic and positive about your company and the opportunity. Develop a clear and specific description of each job role's responsibilities and type of person you want on your team.

You could engage a local recruitment agency to help. There are three types.

- **Retainer agencies** work for a fixed fee and set time. Because of the higher cost, these firms are typically used when your company is hiring for senior-level and executive positions.

- **Contingency agencies** get paid only when their candidate starts working at the firm. These agencies are mostly used for filling junior and administrative positions.
- **Container agencies** are a hybrid of retainer and contingency agencies. They get paid in two installments; when the search project starts and when their candidates start work. This type of agency is designed for mid- to senior-level positions that need to get filled quickly.[3]

When interviewing candidates, be sure to follow U.S. Equal Employment Opportunity Commission (EEOC) guidelines at www.eeoc.gov/overview. Basically, these laws prohibit discriminating against anyone based on age, race, gender, sexual orientation, national origin, color, disability, or religion. Employers are not allowed to show preference for any type of person or discourage anyone from applying for work. For example, a job post that says "Seeking female college graduates" would be illegal, as it shows preference to women with higher educations and discourages men from applying. The guidelines also stipulate that employers are not allowed to ask personal questions during an interview, such as marital status and age.[4]

Hiring Your People

Next, you'll need to create an employee agreement. It's wise to get a local employment lawyer to draft the contracts. In addition to knowing the myriad of federal, state, and local laws and regulations, the attorney can advise how to legally structure the employment relationship.

The most common legal structure is an "at will" relationship where employers hire people without specifying the length of time period. It gives employers tremendous flexibility, as "at will" employees can be terminated at any time without cause or advance notice. Employers in the United States don't legally have to provide severance payment, but generally they give exiting workers two weeks of pay. The downside of "at will" relationships is that employees can quit at any time without giving cause or notice. Nevertheless, it is common practice that workers inform their managers two weeks in advance of leaving.

To create stronger relationships, many companies choose a "for cause" standard with some or all employees. Employers agree they will terminate an employee only when there is a just cause, such as the failure to perform work duties, insubordination, or dishonesty. These agreements are generally given to highly valued employees in management positions or those with special skills.

Many startups and scale-ups choose to hire part-time workers, because of limited financial resources. Generally part-time employees work at least 20 hours per week, although the U.S. Bureau of Labor describes part-time employment as anywhere from one to 34 hours. Your business can then decide whether to offer benefits. This decision is generally based on the ability to attract workers rather than legal mandates.

Another option is to hire people as independent contractors or consultants, particularly for projects with a negotiated flat fee. Independent contractors are responsible for both the individual and employer sides of taxes. These self-employed workers are sometimes called "1099'ers," because employers issue them a 1099 rather than a W-2 statement at the end of the year for tax purposes.

Offering Benefits to Employees

In addition to attractive salaries, you will need to offer certain kinds of benefits to get people to work for your company. In many cases, employees are equally or more concerned about the benefits than salary you offer them. Research by Care.com Workplace Solutions found that 62 percent of American employees would leave their current job for better benefits.[5]

At a minimum, the federal government requires businesses to provide the following six benefits (referred to as *statutory benefits*) to employees:

Social Security benefits ensure that employees will have an income after they retire or if they become permanently disabled. These are funded by taxes paid by both the employee and their employer as payroll deductions.

Medicare benefits provide healthcare coverage to people aged 65 and older or people with certain disabilities or medical conditions. Similar to the Social Security benefit, these are paid by both the employee and their employer as payroll deductions.

Workers' compensation insurance covers the cost of medical care, treatment, rehabilitation, and paid leave or replacement income for employees who are injured or become ill in a situation related to their job.

Unemployment insurance provides partial income replacement for a short time when an employee involuntarily loses their job. Both the employer and employee contribute to unemployment compensation insurance that is administered by state governments.

Health insurance for employees is mandated for organizations with 50 or more full-time employees under the Affordable Care Act of 2010, also known as Obamacare. Employers that don't provide adequate healthcare coverage could face federal penalties. While required only for large organizations, most companies offer health insurance to remain attractive to workers.

Family and medical leave is required by businesses that employ more than 50 people. The Family Medical Leave Act (FMLA) requires companies to provide up to 12 weeks of unpaid leave while still protecting their job security for reasons including the birth of a child, a serious medical condition, or caring for an immediate family member.

In addition to these required benefits, U.S. employers offer additional benefits to attract workers, particularly for managerial and skilled positions in competitive markets and industries. After the first year of the pandemic, in 2021, many employers offered more flexible schedules, mental health coverage, and childcare support to get people back to work. A 2022 Harris Poll of 2,000 U.S. workers found that 51 percent reported that their employers had added new benefits or increased their existing benefits.[6] Among the top added benefits were improved dental and vision care insurance and monies for healthcare and wellness expenses.

Spotlight: Eataly (Italy)

Oscar Farinetti created Eataly with the goal of becoming the world's most recognized Italian food brand.[7] In 2007 he opened a sprawling market in Torino, Italy, where people could eat, shop, and learn. As an article titled "The Supermarket of the Future" reported: "Eataly is an irresistible realization of every food-lover's gluttonous fantasy, paired with guilt-cleansing social conscience—a new combination of grand food hall, farm stand, continuing-education university, and throbbing urban market."[8]

Three years later, Eataly USA, led by Oscar's son Nicola, opened a 50,0000-square-foot market on Fifth Avenue in New York City. It housed dozens of shops with authentic Italian foods and fresh produce as well as seven mini-restaurants, a gelateria, and a vegetable "butcher." While some items were imported, such as parmigiano reggiano cheese, the majority were sourced from local farms, dairies, and other suppliers that met Eataly's high-quality standards.

An important first task for Eataly USA was to hire people since the NYC store needed at least 300 employees to launch. Interviewing candidates was challenging, as employment laws and practices are very different than in Italy. Also, Italians don't separate their work and nonwork lives in the same way Americans do. Co-workers at family-oriented Italian companies tend to be more involved in each other's personal lives.

The Italian management team quickly learned that different professional boundaries and protocols needed to be established from the get-go in order to create a healthy, functional operation in the United States that was true to Eataly's culture and values. Therefore, the first person that Eataly USA hired was an American to run its Human Resource function and to recruit and hire staff.

The first Eataly in the United States was an immediate success, recording $70 million sales in its first year of business.[9] As of March 2022, there are seven Eataly stores across the United States with more than 2,000 employees. An Eataly spokesperson said the company remains mindful of both the legal and cultural differences between the two countries in terms of how business is run and how to build the best possible teams for its American locations.[10]

Note that Eataly successfully entered and scaled in the United States about the same time as Tesco's failed attempt (recounted in the Tesco Case Study in Chapter 9). While both introduced a new supermarket concept, Eataly provided a totally new retail experience with its unique and appealing combination of shops, restaurants, and places to learn about Italian cuisine. Such distinctiveness proved to be the difference between failure and success for Eataly.

Managing American Workers

Managing Americans can be challenging, particularly for managers from countries with hierarchical organizations where decisions are dictated from the top. Getting Americans to follow instructions and direct orders is often a problem for foreign-born managers. According to Lisa DeWaard, managing director and CEO of Hofstede Insights USA, Americans want to be entrusted with the task at hand, yet also be free to do it their own way.[11]

Another problem area is giving American workers criticism and negative feedback, even in formal performance reviews. In general, Americans don't do well with direct criticism.

Scandinavian and European managers have a particularly hard time with this cultural quirk, since they believe being honest is being respectful. In the words of a Dutch executive, "I will tell you the hard facts because I believe you are strong enough to take it and that you will find this most valuable so you can adjust your actions." But when dealing with Americans, the better tactic is to deliver negative feedback along with something positive. Deliver bad news along with good news. Tell an American two or three positive comments about their work before launching into criticism or negative observation.

Most important, however, communication needs to be tailored for each individual person. As you learned in Chapter 9, which presented Hofstede's cross-cultural research, Americans are the most individualist people of any nation. So, as Bruce Buchanan of the Australian unicorn Rokt said, "You gotta know when to drop the hammer to one person and use velvet gloves with another."[12]

Entering and Working with Visas

Visas are legal documents that enable non-U.S. citizens to work and study here for extended periods of time. The process is managed by the federal government's U.S. Citizenship and Immigration Services (USCIS). The U.S. Department of State's website (www.travel.state.gov) publishes extensive information on visas and the process.[13] However, our immigration system is similar to our tax system in a way: Both have many complex laws and regulations, and clear-cut answers are often difficult to find.[14]

There are two types, or categories, of visas. One type are immigration visas, and the other are nonimmigration visas. The first type is for foreigners who want to stay in the country permanently and potentially become U.S. citizens. The nonimmigrant work visa, on the other hand, is for people who want to stay in the country only temporarily. In other words, these visas do not lead to citizenship. So when choosing which type of visa to apply for, remember that a major difference is whether you want to stay in the United States permanently and eventually become a U.S. citizen—or not.

To get an immigration visa, you would first apply for a permanent resident card (known as a *green card*) that allows you to live and work in the United States for as long as you want. These are the steps to getting a green card:

1. Find someone (a "sponsor") to enter an immigrant petition on your behalf. Employers can be sponsors by following PERM regulations to prove that no U.S. citizen worker is available to fill the position and that wages will not be driven down by hiring a foreign worker.
2. After approval, submit an application with the appropriate forms at USCIS in the United States or your foreign embassy.
3. Go for an interview and biometrics screening, where USCIS collects fingerprints and other physical traits for identification purposes.
4. Supply additional information to the USCIS, if they send you a request for evidence (RFE).
5. Await a decision, which the USCIS estimates at four to six months for an employment-sponsored application.[15] However, SHRM's Council for Global Immigration reports the process can take up to six years in H-1B status.[16]

Five years after receiving a green card (three years if you're married to an American), you can apply to become a U.S. citizen, which enables you to get a U.S. passport and vote in U.S. elections. The process of becoming a citizen is called *naturalization*.

The process to get a nonimmigrant visa is generally easier, because there aren't the same limitations on the number granted each year. More than 8.7 million nonimmigrant visas were issued in 2019, although that number dropped to 4 million in 2020 due to COVID.[17] Still the system and process can be confusing, as there are more than 30 types of nonimmigrant visas.

Choosing whether to apply for an immigration visa or a nonimmigration visa is an important decision. Each type has its own laws, issues, and possible outcomes. There's also a relatively new category of visas for investors, the EB-5, that acts a bit differently. It was established during the recession of 1990 to stimulate the U.S. economy, particularly in low-income and rural areas. With an EB-5 visa, investors (and their spouses and unmarried children) can apply for a green card if they invest $800,000 to $1,050,000 in businesses that will create 10 permanent full-time jobs for U.S. workers.[18]

Immigrant Work Visas: A Path to Citizenship

Employment-based (EB) visas are numbered 1 to 4 based on preference in the selection process. For example, EB-1s are awarded before EB-2, EB-3, and EB-4 visas. Given the set number of employment-based visas approved by the U.S. government, applying for one with a higher preference (EB-1 or EB-2) should take less time to obtain than a green card.

EB-1 visas are designated for people with exceptional abilities in the sciences, arts, athletics, education, and business management. Yes, you're first in line for a green card if you're an Oscar-winning actor or an Olympic medal–winning athlete. Distinguished professors and researchers can also apply for an EB-1 if they are wanted by an academic or government institution. If you're a manager or executive of a multinational company, this could be a fast way to get permanence residence.

EB-2 visas are also for people with exceptional abilities in professional fields—such as life sciences and engineering—that require a doctorate or other advanced academic degree. For EB-2 visas, applicants need to have an employer sponsor. In most cases, the employer obtains a labor certification from the Department of Labor (DOL) that there are no able, willing, and qualified U.S. workers for the position. This job requirement could get waived if the candidate is involved in an endeavor considered of "both substantial merit and national importance."[19]

EB-3 visas are designed for skilled workers and professionals who have a minimum of two years' training or experience. It doesn't require an advanced degree. Still candidates need to have an employer sponsor and a full-time job offer. As with EB-2 visas, this requires employers to file an Immigrant Petition for Alien Workers. Also, similar to the other EB visas, spouses and unmarried children under the age of 21 can apply for visas to accompany the worker.

EB-4 visas are available for foreign nationals looking for permanent residence and/or U.S. citizenship in special cases, including religious workers, military and government workers, and special immigrant juveniles.

To learn more about the eligibility requirements for these and all other visas go to the government's website (www.uscis.gov).

Nonimmigrant Work Visas for Temporary Residence in the United States

Nonimmigrant work visas are generally easier to obtain than immigrant visas since they are focused only on business and commerce without the political complication of citizenship, although sometimes people on these visas do apply to become U.S. citizens at a later time.

H-1B visas are designed for skilled professionals with at least a bachelor's degree. Each year 65,000 H-1B visas are issued to foreign nationals for working in a wide range of industries. An additional 20,000 are granted to people who earned a master's degree from an American college or university, and an unlimited number are granted to researchers, professors, and other workers in education. H-1B visas are initially granted for three years and can be extended for another three years. Applicants need to be sponsored by a hiring organization that can show that no qualified U.S. worker is available for the particular job. By law, people working under H-1B visas must receive the same wages, benefits, and working conditions as U.S. citizens. (For an example of a successful use of the H-1B visa, see "Case Study: Petplan" in this chapter.)

L-1 visas are for executives, managers, and people with special skills who work at multinational companies. It is most commonly known as an "intra-company transferee visa." This visa is particularly appropriate when a company wants to transfer people between the United States and their overseas headquarters. Also, multinational companies can file a blanket petition to cover multiple L-1 visas. Typically, L-1 visas are for three years, although foreign executives can get a one-year L-1A to open a new branch or U.S. subsidiary. An appealing aspect of L-1 visas is that spouses and dependents can receive L-2 visas, which permit them to live and work in the United States during the same time period.

E-1 visas were created for individuals from "favored nations" to engage in trade between the United States and foreign enterprises. There are 72 favored nations, so-called because they have treaties for U.S. trade and commerce. E-1 visas are for people doing business through international exchanges of goods, services, and technology. (The USCIS calls them *treaty traders* and lists them on their website.) While there is no dollar amount specified, at least 50 percent of the business activity should take place in the United States. E-1 visas are generally for two years, depending on the treaty nation, and holders can get unlimited two-year extensions. In addition, spouses and dependents can live and legally work in the country.

E-2 visas are for people with investments, or plans to invest, in the United States. Similar to E-1 visas, you are able to renew it indefinitely, and your spouses and dependents can enjoy the same status benefits. The law does not stipulate a dollar amount, but only that the investment needs to be substantial.

E-3 visas are specific to specialty occupation workers from Australia. Per the USCIS definition: "The specialty occupation requires theoretical and practical application of a body of highly specialized knowledge and the attainment of a bachelor's or higher degree in the specific specialty, or its equivalent, as a minimum for entry into the occupation in the United

States." The Australian company Rokt, described in the case study from Chapter 2, benefited from the close relations of our two countries with regard to visas and immigration.

O-1 visas are for people with extraordinary abilities in the arts, sciences, athletics, and business. They do need to prove their achievements and talents with awards or other recognition. Yes, movie and television stars qualify for O-1 visas. The difference from an EB-1 is it doesn't lead to U.S. citizenship. O-2 and O-3 visas are for their assistants and family members.

TN visas allow Canadian and Mexican citizens to work in professional fields in the United States, as negotiated in the North American Free Trade Agreement (NAFTA). It's granted for three years to accountants, engineers, scientists, lawyers, teachers, and other professionals. This nonimmigration status is available to people who have a prearranged full-time or part-time job offer with a U.S. employer. Spouses and children can join on a TN visa, but they can only study in the United States—not work.

F-1 visas allow students to enter the United States to study at an accredited college, university, high school, and other educational institutions. Students can work off-campus after their first academic year under one of three programs: Curricular Practical Training (CPT), Optional Practical Training (OPT), or Science, Technology, Engineering, and Mathematics (STEM) OPT.

J-1 Exchange Visitor Visas are for participation in educational and cultural exchange programs through a designated sponsoring organization in the United States. The exchange visitor categories include teachers, research scholars, physicians, specialists, camp counselors, and au pairs. Many foreign companies use these visas for interns and trainees.

B-1 Business Visitor Visa is a nonimmigrant visa for temporary activities, such as consulting with business associates, attending a conference, settling an estate, or negotiating a contract. Foreign nationals can stay in the United States for six months, and no more than one year if they are granted an extension.

Startup Visas in the Works

There is new momentum for visas that make it easier for foreign-born entrepreneurs to start companies here. In 2021 President Joe Biden restored the International Entrepreneur Parole Rule (IEP), which was created by the Obama administration in 2017. The IER enables foreign-born startup founders who have financial backing from U.S. investors to legally work in the United States for five years. In addition, currently in 2022, the U.S. Congress is considering legislation for more extensive startup visa options.

Immigration lawyer Tahmina Watson is one of the champions for the startup visa. Her law firm, Watson Immigration Law, has been helping foreign-nationals navigate the U.S. immigration system for more than 10 years. Tahmina cautions that there is a lot of preparation and strategy needed for the application process, especially choosing which visa category is most suitable. Still, she is encouraged that people can succeed in our complicated, and sometimes frustrating, system. After emigrating to the United States in 2005, Tahmina became a U.S. citizen in 2011.[20]

Building teams of capable and dedicated employees can be challenging, but once accomplished can be a great competitive advantage. Similarly, navigating the complicated U.S. immigration and visa system can be confusing and frustrating. In both cases, you should seek advice from human resources and legal professionals in the United States. In the next chapter we will examine how to establish market presence in your critical first steps into the U.S. market.

Case Study: Petplan (U.K.)

Chris and Natasha Ashton came to the United States on F-1 visas to study at the Wharton School of Business. Before marriage, Chris was an officer in the U.K. Royal Marines, and Natasha worked for a Greek shipping company. Shortly after arriving in 2001, their Birman cat took ill, which cost them more than $5,000 in veterinary bills. They wanted to purchase pet insurance, but they could find few providers and few affordable options. They were surprised, as these policies were popular in the United Kingdom, where 23 percent of pets were covered by insurance.[21]

With two-thirds of American families owning a pet, the Ashtons saw huge potential for the U.S. market. Over the next two years, the Ashtons created plans for a new pet-focused company. They won the prestigious Wharton Business Plan competition, which awarded them prize money, connections, and national press attention. After graduation, they each were allowed 12 months, under the Optional Practical Training program (OPT), to work on their business idea. They won an exclusive license for the U.S. market from Petplan UK, which in 2003 was the largest pet insurance company in the world. The deal gave Petplan USA access to 30 years of actual data and experienced insurance experts, as well as offering the benefit of an established brand name.

Petplan USA's business quickly grew, and they were able to get H-1B visas as employees. Their H-1B status was later extended for another six years. The Ashtons then petitioned for green cards, which required proving the business was viable and they were uniquely qualified to run it. Natasha was granted a green card based on her experience as a logistics and marketing expert; Chris was awarded a green card as her spouse. Surprisingly, Chris's extensive military experience as an officer in the British Royal Marine commandos was not considered relevant to the petition. Eventually, the couple applied for and became U.S. citizens in 2015, 14 years after arriving in Philadelphia.

(*continued*)

(continued)

Building a Team

The Ashtons always saw Petplan as more than selling pet insurance. Rather, it was a pet health company with employees who cared about pets. They recruited people who were "passionate pet parents" who could empathize with and better serve their customers. Having a positive attitude, strong work ethic, and a desire to improve things were also important qualities to the Ashtons.

As the number of employees grew, Petplan invested in human resource systems to help maintain their strong culture. Even when the company grew to more than 200 people, Chris and Natasha interviewed each employee before they were hired. The company also built an online training portal to provide education and training that was thorough and consistent.

They recognized the importance of hiring industry experts. As Natasha said, "When it came to the insurance side of the business, we did spend money on hiring the very best U.S. lawyers who understood the regulatory environment to help us navigate that side, and that paid off in spades for us."[22] They understood insurance laws intimately and were able to make things happen, which was challenging because each U.S. state had different laws and regulations. And they couldn't market pet insurance the same way in every state. For example, in New York they might be able to offer a $10 gift card, but that was not allowed in Wisconsin and other states.

The Result

Within 10 years, the Ashtons' business grew to $50 million and became the third largest competitor in the pet insurance market.[23] For three years, Petplan USA was listed on

Forbes' list of "America's Most Promising Companies." Eventually, the Ashtons sold the business to a large private equity firm.

Lessons from This Case Study

1. **America wants successful entrepreneurs.** While navigating the U.S. immigration systems wasn't easy for Chris and Natasha, they eventually became full citizens. Their determination and entrepreneurial skills were recognized and rewarded in this country.
2. **Foreigners can see opportunities.** Chris and Natasha were able to see a gap in the U.S. market, particularly compared to the U.K. insurance business. Their outside perspective identified market inefficiencies and opportunities to exploit.
3. **Build a team with people who share your vision.** The Ashtons wanted to create a company for pet owners with people who love pets. Their shared vision led to a culture that delivered valuable products and outstanding customer service.
4. **Get expert help when needed.** The Ashtons partnered with legal experts to navigate the complicated federal government and 50 state legal and regulatory systems in the United States. They wouldn't have been able to build the business without them.

Notes

1. Lawrence Bossidy, AZQuotes.com, Wind and Fly LTD, 2022, www.azquotes.com/quote/587518, Accessed April 30, 2022.
2. U.S. Department of Labor, Consolidated Minimum Wage Table, effective January 1, 2022, Accessed April 30, 2022, www.dol.gov/agencies/whd/mw-consolidated
3. Octopus Ventures, "Question the Questions: Applying Some Socrates to Your U.S. expansion plans," 2018.

4. SelectUSA Investor Guide, U.S. Department of Commerce International Trade Administration, May 2021, p. 65.
5. Patrick Ball, "How Lifestyle Benefits Impact Workplace Productivity," Care.com, Accessed March 11, 2022, benefits.care.com/betterbenefits
6. Megan Leonhard, "The worker shortage is pushing companies to offer more perks and benefits," FORTUNE, February 22, 2022, fortune.com/2022/02/22/worker-shortage-companies-offering-perks-benefits-most-common
7. "Interview with Nicola Farinetti: Waving the Fork for Experience Retail," The Possible, November 2016, www.the-possible.com/interview-nicola-farinetti-eataly-designed-unique-experience-retail
8. Corby Kummer, "The Supermarket of the Future," *The Atlantic*, May 2007, www.theatlantic.com/magazine/archive/2007/05/the-supermarket-of-the-future/305787
9. Glenn Collins, "At Eataly, the Ovens and the Cash Registers Are Hot," *The New York Times*, Aug. 28, 2012, www.nytimes.com/2012/08/29/dining/eataly-exceeds-revenue-predictions.html
10. Conversation with Sara Massarotto, head of Public Relations and Communications at Eataly North America, on March 24, 2021
11. Lisa DeWaard, "The Dread Micromanagement," Hofstede Insights, May 4, 2021, www.linkedin.com/pulse/dread-micromanagement-lisa-dewaard/?trackingId=BR69pC23pzr66%2FN7r7dKsw%3D%3D
12. Conversation with Bruce Buchanan, founder and CEO of Rokt, on March 23, 2021
13. U.S. Department of State - Bureau of Consular Affairs, Accessed May 1, 2022, travel.state.gov/content/travel/en/contact-us/us-visas.html
14. Council for Immigration, "Immigration 101," Society for Human Resource Management, 2018, p.12.
15. U.S. Citizen and Immigration Services, "Historical Median Processing Time for All USCIS Offices for Selected Forms by Fiscal Year," egov.uscis.gov/processing-times/historic-pt
16. Council for Immigration, "Immigration 101," Society for Human Resource Management, 2018, online.fliphtml5.com/fpjw/ilwr/#p=1
17. U.S. Department of State - Bureau of Consular Affairs, Accessed May 1, 2022, travel.state.gov/content/travel/en/legal/visa-law0/visa-statistics/nonimmigrant-visa-statistics.html
18. EB-5 Immigrant Investor Program, U.S. Citizenship and Immigration Services, Accessed May 1, 2022, www.uscis.gov/working-in-the-united-states/permanent-workers/eb-5-immigrant-investor-program
19. Employment-based Immigration: Second Preference EB-2, U.S. Citizenship and Immigration Services, Accessed May 1, 2022, www.uscis.gov/working-in-the-united-states/permanent-workers/employment-based-immigration-second-preference-eb-2

20. Conversation with Tahmina Watson, Watson Immigration Law, on June 7, 2021
21. Zeeshan Haider, "IBISWorld Industry Report – Pet Insurance," IBISWorld, February 2016
22. Conversation with Natasha Ashton, former co-CEO of Petplan, on April 6, 2021
23. Ibid.

11

Establishing Market Presence

"You've got to be in it to win it" is a popular phrase in American vernacular. It's the slogan of the New York state lottery, meant to entice people to bet a few dollars to win millions. The phrase means that in order to succeed at something, you first have to enter the competition. Variations of this message that encourages action and initiative include the following:

"Jump in!"
"Go for the gold!"
"Show them what you're made of!"
"Just do it!"

Now, dear reader, it's your turn to enter the competition. In previous chapters, you learned to form a business entity, develop Go-to-U.S. market strategies, select initial "beachhead" markets, identify sources of capital, build teams, and other steps. Now it's time to bring your business into the U.S. market. For entrepreneurs, it's time to launch your U.S. venture. (Note that even if you're already located here, you still need to create a visible market presence to scale your business. Also noteworthy is that, in the U.S. legal system, the word *you* can refer to either an individual person or an individual business entity, as described in Chapter 7.)

This final chapter of the book will help you develop strategies to establish a U.S. market presence. We start by looking at the initial phase, the opening gambit for entering the market, which is to develop the elements of your product or service's "brand." These are the first steps you'll need to take when trying to capture people's attention and interest in doing business with your company. The chapter then examines marketing and media strategies to turn that attention into business opportunities. Finally, I will wrap up this book with a reflection on the importance of building strong relationships and trust.

Let's begin by looking at the first steps to entering the U.S. market and creating positive first impressions.

Entering the U.S. Stage

Chess masters know the opening is the most important part of the game. After studying their opponents and researching potential strategies, they make their first decisive moves. The opening is the time to test strategies and identify the best approach: bold and aggressive? Or safe and measured? Similarly, in business your opening moves are critical, particularly when entering a new country, marketplace, or community.

If you're part of an international company, you'll need to get the attention of buyers, suppliers, and collaborators. If you're an entrepreneur, you will need to make positive in-roads with potential investors and partners. Simply said, unless you get noticed, no one will consider doing business with you. However, getting noticed in the crowded U.S. market isn't simple. The abundance of digital media doesn't help matters. Every day the average American scans through the equivalent of 300 feet of videos, tweets, images, books, articles, ecommerce, and social media sites, which is approximately the height of the Statue of Liberty![1]

To capture attention at the start, you'll need a strong entrance with clear goals. Theater actors and screen stars know how to enter a scene with the clear goal of introducing their character. They want to be noticed and be recognized as the character they are playing. Acting coaches describe this as arriving with intention and establishing presence. Body language, movement, and dress communicate just as much as spoken words. Sometimes an actor's arrival in the story is announced even before the actor steps on the stage, as other characters talk and share stories about the character. Similarly, Americans will probably learn about you—and create a first impression—before they meet you.

First impressions set the stage for productive relationships and business opportunities. Within seconds people will decide if they are interested or not interested in considering your company and its product. Is it relevant to their needs? Do they trust your organization will deliver on its brand promises? Researchers at Princeton University found that it takes only a tenth of a second to form an impression of a stranger from seeing their face—and even after spending more time with the person, that first impression doesn't change significantly.[2]

Decisions made by first impressions, both good and bad, are difficult to overcome later. Psychologists describe this "first impression bias" as the tendency to base final judgments on information gathered at the beginning. First impressions influence, or anchor, all other information they subsequently receive.

Impressing with Your Brand

Your first impression in the U.S. market will be your brand. What's a brand? The American Marketing Association defines a brand as "a name, term, design, symbol, or any feature that indicates a seller's goods or services as distinct from other sellers."[3] That definition is too narrow, however; it doesn't capture all of the ways that brands resonate with people. Think of your experience going to a restaurant in a new city. Certainly, the name and signage made a strong first impression. Were you impressed with the décor and atmosphere? Were the aromas pleasant and the noise level acceptable? Did you feel welcomed and valued by the staff? If not, you might leave and try another restaurant.

So your brand needs to be clear and compelling—not to everyone, just the people who are important for your business: potential customers, business partners, suppliers, employees, investors, and other influential people. American consumers are cautious about buying products from unknown companies, particularly since they generally have many options to choose from. The case study on Hyundai at the end of this chapter tells how the Korean company established its brand before selling any automobiles.

According to Kai D. Wright, Columbia University professor and former global consulting partner at Ogilvy, "Brand is now how the consumer remembers you."[4] In his book *Follow the Feeling*, Wright identifies five areas where brands find ways to connect with audiences.

- **Lexicon Triggers.** Words, phrases, and names are powerful tools for creating distinct brand identities. They create emotions that trigger thoughts and actions. Brand names communicate much about the product. Even made-up, invented names, such as Verizon and Häagen-Dazs, convey strong messages. Taglines, hashtags, and product stories are also part of the lexicon that marketers use to create and promote brands.
- **Audio Cues.** Music, sounds, and rhythm are effective tools for creating brand identity. These sensory elements create strong emotions and reactions. In establishing its luxury brand, Nordstrom distinguished its upscale retail stores by having live music on-site, played by a concert pianist. The "startup" sound of a Netflix video or the roar of a Harley Davidson motorcycle introduce their brand each time their products are used.
- **Visual Stimuli.** Symbols, shapes, logos, and colors are distinct elements in virtually all brands. Visual images communicate much faster, and often more expressively, than spoken or written words. M.I.T. scientists discovered the human mind process images in 13 milliseconds, much less than the time it takes to blink.[5] With digital and social media, visual images can spread in the blink of an eye, too.
- **Experience Drivers.** People's sensations, feelings, and behavioral responses are key to making an encounter

with a brand positive and memorable. BMW built its U.S. brand by promising and delivering an "ultimate driving experience." Financial services firms, including banks and investment advisors, know their brand's reputation is greatly determined by meeting or exceeding consumers' expectations. In the best cases, their customers will become advocates for the brand, telling others about it at social gatherings and on social media.

- **Culture Connections.** The values, behaviors, and rituals of companies have become increasing important to their brand reputation. This includes how it aligns with its audience on political and societal issues. Consumers now want to do business with companies that share their values on topics including sustainability, socio-economics, and environmental issues. They expect the purpose of the organization to be more than just selling products and making profits. According to a 2021 study: 73 percent of U.S. consumers think brands must act for the good of society and the planet, with 53 percent saying they would pay more for brands that take a stand on these issues.[6]

Generating Awareness and Interest

It's not enough to make a great product with a strong brand, get it on the shelf in a U.S. store, and hope it will sell itself. If people in the market have never heard of it, then you'll need to invest in creating awareness with potential buyers and consumers. Otherwise, customers probably won't notice or consider your product when they arrive at the store or online shopping website.

If you're selling a business product or service, you'll need to create awareness among business executives and procurement officers before any sale can be made. According to the Corporate Executive Board, 77 percent of business-to-business (B2B) purchasers said they would not even speak to a salesperson until they had done their own research about the product or service in question.[7] For large purchases, businesses send a request for proposal (RFP) to a select group of suppliers and vendors. The document asks for qualifications and financial information to make their purchase decisions. If the purchaser isn't aware of your company and business solution, there is little chance you'll get an RFP.

Internet search engines and Amazon have made it incredibly easy for people to investigate options, learn about brands, and read online ratings and reviews before making purchase decisions. In virtually every product category—from olive oil and running shoes to life insurance and automobiles—awareness is generated online early in a consumer's buying journey. According to a GE Capital Retail Bank study, 81 percent of retail shoppers conduct online research before buying.[8] This online research is why many food companies offer recipes using their ingredients on mobile websites and apps: they know that people often plan their menus outside their kitchens. Mobile technology has made the research even easier. Most Americans (85 percent) have smartphones with Internet access, and they spend more than five hours a day on their devices for nonwork–related purposes.[9]

Once they discover an item or learn a fact on the Internet, it is difficult for people to change their opinions later. Basically, people trust themselves a lot more than they trust other people. Psychologists call this the *confidence effect*. Therefore, whatever people discover for themselves on the Web, they'll consider that more credible and more true than information received directly from other people and media. That's why it is critical to get the attention of potential audiences early in their purchase journeys.

Google has built the largest advertising company in the world because it provides access to the precise moment when people are interested in a product or service: when they go to search online about it or a related topic. Jim Lecinski, former Google executive and now associate professor at Northwestern University, coined the term *zero moment of truth* (ZMOT). This is the moment a person recognizes a need and seeks information. Often this recognition is triggered by a stimulus, such as an advertisement, social post, newspaper article, or comment from a friend or colleague. Later the person decides whether to purchase a product when they encounter it in a store or shopping website, which is called the *first moment of truth*. Importantly, the decision to purchase is heavily influenced by the information and first impressions gleaned through online and offline research.

Awareness increases when the product or brand is more discoverable by search engines, such as Google. Lecinski recommends using the Google Trends online tool to see what consumers are wanting to know at the ZMOT.[10] For example, they might be inquiring, "What's the best imported organic olive oil?" Next is to develop articles and other content featured on your website. This will help your brand or product show up in Google search results for these ZMOTs. He also recommends investigating if demand already exists for a brand like yours. People may already be searching for "best melting cheese from France." If that's the case, then you need to show up in Google search results to capture that existing demand. This can be accomplished by hiring digital experts to conduct a website optimization procedure for you.

Be forewarned that the process of becoming "discoverable" on Google and other search engines is fairly lengthy, however. Digital marketing experts estimate that it takes six to eight months for website optimization and content marketing strategies to start to return results. Therefore, you should look into faster ways to stimulate demand and gain traction through other marketing activities and media channels, as described next.

Getting Traction in the U.S. Market

If you're looking to scale your business, getting off to a fast start is all-important. Early momentum will demonstrate your product and company's viability to investors, distributors, and cautious buyers. Advertising, public relations, or other marketing and promotion activities can generate awareness and interest faster. Which media and tactics to use will depend on many factors and variables, such as the industry and market dynamics. The competitive landscape, size of the target market, and competitive activity also will influence the marketing strategies and tactics.

Certainly, the amount of money you can invest will greatly determine the size and scope of the marketing effort. Many international companies complain that the cost of marketing and advertising is significantly higher in the United States than other countries. This is true, which means that companies need to focus their marketing efforts on specific audiences with realistic objectives.

When the Jamaican beer company Red Stripe looked to expand in the United States in the early 2000s, it focused its advertising and music concert promotions in just a few cities. Brand strategist Ole Pedersen said it was cost effective and created a buzz with influential communities. This social diffusion strategy took pains not to appear corporate or promotional, in line with the subversive, no-frills essence of the brand. An identity famously celebrated in Red Stripe's advertising slogan "Hooray, beer!"[11]

Which media you use is an important consideration. Advertising and marketing agencies try to maximize the impact by crafting integrated campaigns using multiple media and tactics. Many utilize the PESO communications model to identify the appropriate media and interactions. The acronym stands for "paid," "earned," "shared," and "owned" media. Let's look at each of these aspects.

Paid media is any channel for marketing content or messages where the advertiser must pay a fee. Basically, companies pay for the right to deliver their message to the media's audience. This includes traditional media, including television, radio, outdoor billboards, and print publications. Paid media placements are available in streaming video, websites, social media, electronic newsletters, and other digital vehicles.

Earned media is any mentions, articles, or images that appear without a cost to the company. These free placements are generally the result of PR professionals contacting the media outlets with press releases and newsworthy information. Earned media also includes reviews and mentions on the websites of investors, industry analysts, and bloggers.

Shared media refers to all content and comments about brands and products distributed by people in online communities, including Facebook, Twitter, and Instagram. Brands can initiate this free channel distribution by posting "share-worthy" content. Some employ paid influencers to post about their brands, such as how cosmetic companies pay supermodels to start the sharing. While shared media can amplify a brand's visibility, companies can't control the distribution and volume.

Owned media is hosted and published by a company. It includes the company's websites, blogs, webinars, videos, and printed publications. It also includes its Facebook, Instagram, Twitter, and LinkedIn pages. Some companies create their own channel on YouTube for posting videos. Offline owned media might include printed brochures and publications, branded content, outdoor billboards, and store displays.

For example, an Israeli cybersecurity company needed to generate awareness and interest for its advanced threat detection systems. The three-year-old company recently received $50 million in venture capital to expand its U.S. sales and marketing activities. The funding was secured after its Chicago office won a long-term contract with a major financial services firm. With the help of local marketing agencies, it launched an integrated campaign using the PESO model. **Owned** media included a new website with articles, facts, and keywords around cybersecurity to be discovered on Google and other search engines. For **earned** media, they sent press releases and scheduled interviews for the founders with industry reporters and bloggers. On **paid** media it launched a digital advertising campaign targeted to information technology (IT) executives. **Shared** media was generated with share-worthy social media posts about security threats identified by their system. In addition, the Israeli company exhibited at several cybersecurity conferences.

Conferences and trade shows don't quite fit into the PESO model, but they should be considered. There you can meet lots of industry people, check out competitors, and get traction with potential customers. Virtually every industry, from automobiles to video technology, has at least one major event each year. The Consumer Electronics Show, held every January in Las Vegas, had more than 171,000 attendees with 4,419 exhibiting companies in 2020.[12] During the COVID pandemic, many trade shows turned into interactive digital events, but most plan to return to full, in-person events.

Many international companies, particularly in technology and B2B industries, find that exhibiting at U.S. conferences and trade shows is an effective way to enter the market. It can be costly, however, as fees for exhibitor space, booth signage, and product brochures are significant. Also, there is the cost for travel and expenses of employees to be present at the booth. Still, such shows and conferences could be a great way to announce your commitment and capabilities to the industry and market.

If you are just starting to look at expanding to the United States, you should consider going to the annual SelectUSA conference. It's run by the U.S. Department of Commerce's International Trade Administration to help international companies invest and bring their businesses here. It's a good place to meet economic development organizations from across the country as well as investors and service providers.

Bill Kenney, founder of My Expo & Event Team (MEET) and Soft Land Partners, says, "Effective preparation is 90 percent of winning the race; this is especially true with SelectUSA."[13] He recommends researching the exhibitors and attendees before the event to target your efforts. If possible, try to set up meetings in advance of the conference. Also, he says, have a very clear pitch and value proposition. Be prepared with documents, such as company overviews, investor summaries, and product brochures. Then be sure to follow up and nurture the relationships started at the event.

Building Strong Relationships

An essential element to being successful in the United States is your ability to establish positive relationships built on a foundation of trust and mutual respect. Consumers need to trust that your products will deliver the promised value. Investors need to trust that you will deliver a solid return on their investment (ROI). Suppliers need to trust that you will pay your bills. Employees need to trust your company's values and vision. Likewise, you need to be able to trust the integrity and commitment of those people.

Dozens of the international businesspeople I interviewed said they were able to build those relationships here. Of course, they spoke about needing to overcome cultural differences. A few encountered some disreputable characters. But on the whole, people felt that Americans are trusting, trustworthy, and generous. Americans speak openly and are straightforward about wanting "win-win" arrangements.

Helio Fred Garcia, president of Logos Consulting Group, believes that trust is the most important element in business.[14] His firm specializes in crisis management that restores trust for companies and leaders with their stakeholders and the general public if necessary. He explains there are three related, but distinct, drivers of trust.

> **Promises kept.** This builds and reinforces trust in people. These can be explicit promises, such as, "We'll take care of you." They can also be implicit promises, such as a brand's offer of quality, value, or support. Trust falls if we are seen to break promises.
>
> **Expectations met.** This increases trust, and trust falls when expectations have not been met. These expectations could be formally stated by law, verbal agreements, or contracts. Expectations could also be set by our prior

behavior, or expectations set by society, such as #MeToo or diversity, equity, and inclusion (DEI) behaviors and practices.

Values lived. Trust arises when our stated values are the *lived experience* of other people in the relationship. Trust falls when people see or experience us behaving contrary to those values. Companies often issue a statement of values as a kind of promise that sets an expectation.

Here is an example of a company, MediaMint, that built its U.S. business through strong relationships with U.S. companies based on trust and mutual respect.

Spotlight: MediaMint (India)

Aditya Vuchi came to the United States from India to study engineering at West Virginia University. After graduating, he joined the Tribal Fusion agency in Silicon Valley to build technologies that create, distribute, and track the performance of digital advertising. Four years later Aditya was promoted to director of Global Operations, and he built a highly efficient "back office" operation in India to deliver complex digital advertising campaigns for Tribal Fusion's clients.

Entrepreneurs at heart, Aditya and his wife, software engineer Neelima Marupuru, saw the skyrocketing growth in digital advertising. U.S. digital advertising revenues were $26 billion at that time in 2010, and in 10 years they grew to $140 billion.[15] The couple founded MediaMint in Hyderabad, India, with a U.S. subsidiary based in San Francisco. Their goal was to be a valued and trusted business partner to the world's biggest advertisers and media companies.

The couple hired Jason Riback, an operations expert from McKinsey & Co., as MediaMint's president to build a world-class organization focused on client service and execution. Jason knew that business executives in the United States would need convincing to trust their critical operations to an unknown, foreign company. MediaMint started by asking for small projects and then over-delivering with flawless execution and extensive performance reporting. Clients loved this, since it meant they could show their bosses how their operation was running efficiently and effectively. MediaMint's mantra to its clients? "It's our job to earn your business every day."[16]

MediaMint grew by focusing on building strong client relationships and exceeding their expectations for flexibility, scalability, and efficiency. In 2022 the company was purchased by Brightcom Group for a reported $75 million in cash and stock. At the time, the company employed more than 1,300 people and was servicing clients including Expedia, Pinterest, The New York Times, and Netflix.[17]

Final Notes of Advice

During my research for this book, I was asked many times for advice on marketing products and services in the United States. As I've mentioned, there are no rules or formulas because every industry, every company, every market, and every situation is different. Still, I wouldn't be fulfilling my obligations as an author, consultant, and teacher if I didn't provide some general recommendations. What follows are eight things I've observed to be true:

Tailor brands for the U.S. market. Don't assume the brand used in your home country will be appropriate. There might be negative connotations to the image, name, or brand message. Companies from the United Kingdom and other English-speaking countries have had to customize their websites and product literature to connect with American audiences.

Be authentic. Americans don't like imitations; they prefer the real stuff, the originals. In this regard, foreigners have a competitive advantage, as they can introduce authentic products, recipes, and designs from their home country. Americans love to discover and try new things, which they can boast about to their friends—as in, "Hey, I just found this amazing wine from Chile!"

Be noteworthy and memorable. The United States is a crowded market with many options for consumers and business buyers. Therefore, you need to enter the competition by being new and interesting—standing out, worth noticing and talking about, exceptional. Seth Godin calls this being remarkable: "It's a purple cow. Boring stuff is invisible. It's a brown cow."[18]

Research U.S. audiences. Consumers look for brands that can fulfill their needs and desires. Market research can uncover these requirements among groups of consumers. Ideally, you'll conduct market research in the United States with a large sample size. At the very least you should conduct informal interviews for qualitative information and insights. Later, refine your marketing activities based on the new research and market performance.

Hire local experts. It's wise to engage people living in the United States to tailor branding and craft marketing. It's necessary to demonstrate that you understand consumers' problems and needs by speaking their language, using their idioms, and respecting their culture. Business-to-business customers want to see a commitment to the United States that can be demonstrated with a local presence. Several U.K companies have made the mistake of not creating a U.S.-specific website, assuming instead: "Well, it's all the same language." But that attitude misses the many key differences in spelling, idioms, humor, tastes, and other preferences between those countries lying across the ocean from one another.

Create integrated marketing. Marketing activities should include paid, earned, and owned media that can be amplified with shared media generated by consumers, influencers, and others. These should be timed appropriately so the activities can work together. This is especially true when marketing on a tight budget. That means great advertising and marketing communications pointing to a strong website and social pages, which include images and press articles that can be shared. This is how big ideas can generate big results at little cost.

Get warm introductions. A referral from someone that your target customers and clients trust and whose judgment they respect is all-important. A warm introduction (via email or in person) will often get you a meeting, or at least a phone call, in which you can pitch your story or your ask. For international businesses entering business-to-business and other fields, it's valuable to find locals who can become part of your team. People with local connections will save you months of calling and follow-up messages on prospective customers.

Test, test, test. Try multiple marketing strategies and tactics. See which are most promising. No doubt your original ideas will need to be adapted, tweaked, or pivoted when you launch them in the United States. Entrepreneurs should have a nimble mindset (test, learn, adjust) rather than a fixed mindset ("These people just don't understand our solution yet").

Looking Forward

It's my sincere hope that after reading this book you feel better prepared to enter and scale in U.S. markets. At the very least, you can enter with "eyes wide open" and armed with questions that need to be investigated. Before you close this book, have a look at an inspiring case study of an unknown company, Hyundai, that became the bestselling automobile brand in America its first year. From that auspicious start, it scaled its U.S. business with manufacturing, design, research, and administrative facilities in Alabama, California, and Michigan. Then, in the appendixes, you'll find three checklists that should be helpful on your journey.

In closing, let me say that our country truly is a place where dreams can come true. Yes, the path can be difficult, and some groups and individuals have inequitable advantages. But you also will find many helpful people, just like me, who are rooting for you to be successful.

So, please bring your business and your talents to the United States. As we say here, "I look forward to seeing you."

Case Study: Hyundai (South Korea)

Hyundai was founded by Chung Ju Yang who was born to a poor farming family in North Korea. At the age of 18, he set off to Seoul to find a better life. After laboring in construction and railway jobs, he landed a job as a deliveryman in a rice store where he impressed the owner with his business skills. At 22, Chung became the owner of the rice store. However, he was forced to close it by Japanese occupation forces in 1939. After the liberation of Korea in WWII, Chung started an automobile repair business and did some work on U.S. Army trucks. Within three years, his business had 70 employees.

After the liberation of Korea in 1946, Chung started his company, Hyundai Engineering and Construction, because he knew his country would need to rebuild its infrastructure. It won major government contracts to build roads, dams, and highways. It also won contracts with the U.S. military for buildings and facilities. Despite a lack of experience in shipbuilding, he persuaded a customer to build a ship for tens of millions of dollars. Today Hyundai

Heavy Industries is the largest ship builder in the world.

Chung explained his success: "We succeeded because our people devoted their enterprising spirits. They used the force of the minds. Conviction creates indomitable efforts. This is the key to miracles. . . . Man's potential is limitless."[19]

Chung dreamed of doing business in the United States, which grew from his positive relationship with Americans after WWII. It further developed when Hyundai began assembling automobiles for the Ford Motor Company in 1970. His first entry into the U.S. market came in 1986 with the Hyundai Excel. The car came in either a two- or four-door sedan version with a price range of $4,995 to $6,445. That was about half the price of most new cars; a four-door sedan from General Motors Pontiac cost $12,400.

But having a low price was not a guarantee of success. Americans were skeptical of foreign cars with low prices. A few years earlier, a Yugoslavian company introduced the Yugo that sold for around $4,000. However, it was slow, crawling to 60 miles per hour (mph) in 14 seconds, and it had major mechanical issues. *Car and Driver* magazine dubbed it "the worst car in history." Many Americans called it the "NoGo."

A major problem was name recognition: At the time in the 1980s, few people in the United States had ever heard of Hyundai. In marketing terms, its brand recognition was zero. In addition, Americans didn't know how to pronounce the company name. One critic said it sounded like "high and dry," which in the American vernacular means being in a desperate situation with little resources. Certainly, this wasn't good for an automobile company.

Hyundai's first move into the United States was to hire Backer & Spielvogel Advertising. The agency set out

(*continued*)

(*continued*)

to establish Hyundai as a global manufacturing company that could be trusted to produce a good car. It knew Americans would first need to be sold on Hyundai before they would consider buying its low-priced automobiles. The agency created television commercials, billboards, and print advertisements that introduced Hyundai as an industrial leader. One showed Hyundai-built ships conquering rough ocean waters. Another presented towering buildings being built with Hyundai equipment. The advertising ran for three or four months without any mention of the fact that Hyundai also produced automobiles.

After the American public became aware of Hyundai and its industrial prowess, the agency launched advertisements introducing the cars. Then after three months or so, it started to advertise the Hyundai Excel as a new, smart choice. The advertising was noteworthy and memorable. One television commercial featured a man driving home from the Hyundai dealer with two cars. He'd drive about 100 yards in one car. Stop. And scuttle back to the second car to drive it forward 100 yards. This was meant to demonstrate that you could buy two Hyundai's for the price of a single American car.

The strategy worked: The Excel was the fastest selling new car launch ever. In the first year, Hyundai sold more than 100,000 cars. It also signed on many American businesspeople who wanted to open Hyundai automobile sales and service dealerships. In 2021, Hyundai's 820 dealerships sold more than 738,000 vehicles. Nearly half were built at the Hyundai factory in Alabama. Its U.S. operations contribute more than 94,000 private-sector jobs with a total impact of $7 billion to the U.S. economy.[20]

Lessons from This Case Study

1. **Establish credibility.** Americans won't consider buying products or services from a company they don't know and don't trust. Hyundai needed to establish itself in the U.S. market as a strong and capable manufacturing company. It needed a strong brand.
2. **Make a strong entrance.** You can't go into an American market timidly. Hyundai got people's attention and interest with smart marketing and a good story. If you can't afford to reach the entire country, focus on making a strong entrance in one region or city and then expanding to other markets.
3. **Hire local experts.** The U.S. market is complex and challenging. Consumers and business buyers are skeptical and demanding. Therefore, it's wise to hire business consultants and marketing experts with experience and local knowledge.
4. **Success is attainable.** International companies that successfully enter the U.S. experience many years of sustained growth and profitability. Why? Because along with the difficulties and challenges, companies learn, grow, and develop muscles that ultimately attract top talent.

Notes

1. Kai D. Wright, *Follow the Feeling; Brand building in a noisy world* (Hoboken, New Jersey: John Wiley & Sons, 2019), p. 27.
2. Eric Wargo, "How Many Seconds to a First Impression?" *APS Observer* 19, July 2006, www.psychologicalscience.org/observer/how-many-seconds-to-a-first-impression
3. "Branding," *American Marketing Association* (blog), Accessed April 1, 2022, www.ama.org/topics/branding
4. Kai D. Wright, *Follow the Feeling; Brand building in a noisy world* (Hoboken, New Jersey: John Wiley & Sons, 2019), p. 8.
5. Anne Trafton, *MIT News,* Massachusetts Institute of Technology, January 16, 2014, news.mit.edu/2014/in-the-blink-of-an-eye-0116

6. Kyle O'Brien, "Havas' Meaningful Brands Survey Finds Consumers are Cynical," ADWEEK, May 24, 2021, www.adweek.com/agencies/brands-are-facing-the-age-of-cynicism-from-skeptical-consumers
7. "149 Eye-Opening Sales Stats to Consider in 2022 (By Category)," SPOTIO, December 6, 2021, spotio.com/blog/sales-statistics
8. Derek Andersen, "33 Statistics Retail Marketers Need to Know for 2021," July 19, 2021, www.invoca.com/blog/retail-marketing-statistics
9. "Time Spent on Average on a Smartphone in the U.S. 2021," Statista, Accessed April 8, 2022, www-statista-com.ezproxy.cul.columbia.edu/statistics/1045353/mobile-device-daily-usage-time-in-the-us
10. Conversations with Jim Lecinski, associate professor at Northwestern University and former Google executive, on March 18 and 23, 2022
11. Conversation with Ole Pedersen on April 1, 2022
12. "2020-Ces-Attendance-Audit-summary.Pdf," Consumer Electronics Show, cdn.ces.tech/ces/media/pdfs/2020-ces-attendance-audit-summary.pdf
13. Conversation with Bill Kenney on March 30, 2021
14. "Leaders Understanding Trust in Times of Change," n.d., Communication Intelligence, Accessed April 6, 2022, ci-magazine.com/home/leaders-best-understanding-trust-in-times-of-change
15. iab Report, "IAB Full Year 2010 0413 Final," www.iab.com/wp-content/uploads/2015/05/IAB_Full_year_2010_0413_Final.pdf
16. Conversation with Jason Riback, president of MediaMint, on April 19, 2021
17. Telanganatoday, "Hyderabad-based Brightcom acquires MediaMint for Rs 566 crore," Telangana Today, December 7, 2021.
18. Seth Godin, *Purple Cow; Transform Your Business By Being Remarkable* (New York: Portfolio, 2003), p. 8.
19. Richard M. Steers, *Made in Korea: Chung Ju Yung and the Rise of Hyundai* (New York: Routledge,1999), pp. 1–5.
20. Press Release, Hyundai, November 11, 2011, www.hyundai.com/worldwide/en/company/newsroom/hyundai%25E2%2580%2599s-u.s.-operations-contribute-more-than-94%252C000-private-sector-jobs-and-total-impact-of-%25247-billion-to-national-economy-0000001069

Appendix A: Go-to-U.S. Market Readiness Checklist

Leadership

1. Is senior management committed to U.S. entry and/or expansion?
2. Do leaders have knowledge and experience in U.S. markets?
3. What is your organization's goal (or purpose)?
4. What are the SMART objectives for this initiative?
5. How will you measure performance against the SMART objectives?

Product/Service

1. What is the size of the market for the product or service (i.e., total addressable market)?
2. What solutions or benefits will you be filling (i.e., product-customer-market-fit)?
3. Will the product/service need to be modified for the U.S. market (i.e., specifications, package)?
4. What are the estimated sales for the United States in year 1 and year 2?
5. How will you meet the demand (i.e., production capacity, new factory, outsource)?
6. How will you distribute products (i.e., distributors, direct to consumers)?

Financing

1. What are the projected revenue, costs, and cash flow for the U.S. business?
2. What funding will be needed for U.S. expansion?
3. Where will funding come from?
4. How will you handle the U.S. banking needs?
5. How will you handle the U.S. accounting activities?

People/Talent/Human Resources

1. What current employees will be used for the U.S. market?
2. What immigration and visa issues exist?
3. What new roles will need to be filled for the U.S. market?
4. How will you manage the human resources function in the United States?
5. What health, insurance, and other benefits will be required?
6. Will language or cultural training be needed?

Legal and Tax

1. Have you established the proper legal entity for the new market?
2. What U.S. legal counsel have you established?
3. What regulatory requirements may affect your business?
4. What intellectual property (IP) rights will need to be secured (i.e., trademarks)?
5. What product liability issues might you encounter?
6. What are the federal, state, and local municipality taxes?

Marketing and Sales

1. Who are the current and potential competitors?
2. How will you differentiate your product/service (i.e., value proposition)?

3. How will you sell products/services (i.e., sales representatives, agents, dealers)?
4. What marketing is required to generate awareness and interest?
5. How will you service customers and clients (i.e., U.S. service people)?
6. Will marketing and sales materials need to be translated and localized?
7. What is the estimated budget for marketing?

Appendix B: Startup in U.S. Readiness Checklist

Leadership

1. Are the founders committed to launching in the United States?
2. Do the founders and key executives have knowledge and experience in U.S. markets?
3. What is your organization's goal (or purpose)?
4. What are the SMART objectives for this venture?
5. How will you measure performance against the SMART objectives?

Product/Service

1. What is the size of the market for the product or service (i.e., total addressable market)?
2. What is the stage of product development (i.e., concept, initial product release [IPR], minimum viable product [MVP], minimum viable repeatable [MVR])?
3. Have you determined product-customer-market-fit?
4. What are the estimated sales for the United States in year 1 and year 2?
5. How will you meet the demand (i.e., produce internally, outsource, joint venture)?
6. How will you distribute products (i.e., distributors, direct to consumers)?

Financing

1. What are the projected revenue, costs, and cash flow for startup?
2. What funding will be needed for the launch and early years?
3. Where will you secure funding (i.e., angel investor, VC, bank)?
4. How will you set up banking relationship in the United States?
5. How will you handle U.S. accounting activities?

People/Talent/Human Resources

1. What current employees will be used for the U.S. market?
2. What immigration and visa issues exist?
3. What new roles will need be filled for the U.S. market?
4. How will you manage the human resources function in the United States?
5. What health, insurance, and other benefits will be required?
6. Will language or cultural training be needed?

Legal and Tax

1. Have you established the proper legal entity for the new market?
2. Have you established a U.S. legal counsel?
3. What regulatory requirements may affect your business?
4. What intellectual property (IP) rights will need to be secured (i.e., trademarks)?
5. What product liability issues might you encounter?
6. What are the federal, state, and local municipality taxes?

Marketing and Sales

1. Have you identified and researched potential customers?
2. How will you differentiate your product/service (i.e., value proposition)?
3. How will you sell products/services (i.e., sales representatives, agents, dealers)?
4. Have you calculated the customer acquisition cost?
5. How will you service customers and clients (i.e., U.S. service people)?
6. Who are the current and potential competitors?
7. What is the estimated budget to launch the brand and enter the United States for marketing?

Appendix C: Legal Checklist

Business Formation

1. What U.S. legal counsel have you engaged?
2. What type of entity will you establish (C corp or LLC)?
3. In which U.S. state do you want to form the business entity?
4. Do you want to attract and secure funds from outside investors? (If yes, then strongly consider establishing your business entity in Delaware.)
5. Have you identified the capital amount required for the formation of the entity (legal minimum and business needs)?
6. Have you identified a registered agent in that state to accept service of process and official mail?
7. If the owner is a non-U.S. individual or corporation, have you filed a foreign investment report with the U.S. Department of Commerce (required within 45 days of formation)?
8. Have you created Articles of Incorporation (C corp) or Articles of Organization (LLC)?
9. Have you registered with other U.S. states where you will be doing business?
10. Have you consulted with an accountant to ensure there are no surprises on global tax planning?
11. Do you know who will be authorized to represent the company and be appointed as officers, directors, or managers (foreign team members or local employees)?

Employment

1. Have you secured proper visas for people to work in the United States?

2. Have you applied for a federal employer identification number (FEIN)?
3. Have you created employment contracts specific to the states where they will work?
4. Have you created a noncompete agreement for employees, consultants, and temporary workers? (Check if it's allowed in state where employees will work.)

Intellectual Property

1. Have you searched the U.S. Patent and Trademark Office website to see if your brand name and other trademarks are available?
2. Have you registered your brand name and other trademarks with the USPTO?
3. Have you started to use the ™ symbol for your trademark?
4. Once the trademark is registered, are you using ® symbol both online and in printed materials?
5. Have you considered applying for a U.S. patent for any invention or discovery?
6. Have you created an agreement that assigns to the company any intellectual property created by an employee or contract worker during the course of their employment there? (This is often called an *assignment of inventions* or *ownership of discoveries* agreement.)
7. Are you marking all original works (books, computer code, movies, etc.) registered with © and the year of creation to show they are copyright protected?

Other Legal Considerations

1. What federal, state, and local laws and regulations exist for your category of business?
2. What product liability issues might you encounter?
3. Have you created U.S. contracts for product and service sales?

4. Have you created written intercompany agreements?
5. For software-as-a-service (SaaS) companies, have you created U.S.-style licensing service documents? (You need to determine if the license is from the parent, U.S. subsidiary, or other, depending on global tax strategy and liability considerations.)
6. If marketing and other functions are being provided by the parent company, will they be billed using a cost-plus model or as a licensing entity?
7. Will data privacy laws allow you to collect customer and user data?

Glossary

Term	Definition
accelerators	A type of business incubator that provides startup teams with working space, mentorship, and introductions to industry experts and investors, typically in exchange for equity in the startup.
amortization	In corporate accounting, the deduction of capital expenses over the useful life of the asset, such as a piece of equipment or a patent.
angel investor	An accredited investor who invests personal capital in early-stage, potentially high-growth companies.
bill of lading	A document issued by a carrier that acknowledges receipt of cargo (freight) and their obligation to deliver it in good condition to the person (or company) consigning the goods.
boot-strapping	Funding a company only by reinvesting initial profits. The term comes from "pulling yourself up by your own bootsteps."
burn rate	The monthly negative cash flow experienced by a startup before it begins to turn a profit.
capital markets	Exchanges where money is channeled between suppliers—individuals or institutions with capital to lend or invest—and companies in need of capital.
capital structure	The combination of debt and equity used by a company to fund its operations and growth.
commercial loan	A loan that is extended to a business by a bank or other financial institutions.
common stock	Security that represents an ownership share in a company and holds a voting right. In the event of a liquidation of assets, creditors and preferred stockholders get paid before common stockholders.

compliance risk An organization's potential exposure to legal penalties, financial forfeiture, and material loss resulting from its failure to act in accordance with industry laws and regulations, internal policies, or prescribed best practices. This is also known as *integrity risk*.

corporate governance The system of checks and balances to make organizations' directors and managers more accountable and better aligned with stakeholder interests.

corporate social responsibility (CSR) Voluntary actions by organizations to benefit communities and have a positive influence on the world.

crowdfunding Online platforms that connect people investing small sums with for-profit and nonprofit organizations looking for capital.

DACA Deferred Action for Childhood Arrivals; a form of temporary administrative relief from deportation.

dealer Organization that buys products to sell either directly to customers or to retailers. Generally, dealers serve a smaller region than distributors.

debt service The cash required to pay back the principal and interest of outstanding debt for a particular period of time.

distributor Organization that purchases products directly from manufacturers and sells them to dealers and retailers for eventual sale to customers.

economic development organization (EDO) Organization engaged in developing business activity within a city, state, or region. EDOs often try to attract international companies.

emigrant Person who leaves their own country to settle permanently in another country.

employee identification number (EIN) A unique identification that is assigned to a business to ensure it can be identified by the U.S. Internal Revenue Service.

excise taxes Sales taxes levied on specific goods. Typically, these are issued by states on "vice" items, such as liquor, cigarettes, and gasoline.

expat or expatriate Person who lives outside their native country.

foreigner Person belonging to or owing allegiance to a foreign country.

goal	Outcome statement that defines what an organization or person wants to accomplish. Lafley and Martin call it a "winning aspiration."
green card or permanent resident card	Document that enables non-U.S. citizen to live and work in the United States for as long as they want.
green-field investment	Investment for building new factories and facilities rather than purchasing existing ones.
gross domestic product (GDP)	The market value of all goods produced over a period of time, typically a year. This is widely seen as an indicator of a country's economic health.
immigrant visa	Visa for people intending to become U.S. citizens. This includes employment-based visas such as EB-1, EB-2, EB-3, EB-4, and EB-5.
initial public offering (IPO)	When a company (called the *issuer*) issues common stock or shares to the public for the first time, essentially relinquishing its status as a private entity.
internationalization	Making products as flexible as possible, creating a solid basis for localization and translation.
joint venture	A commercial enterprise undertaken by two or more businesses pooling their resources and expertise to achieve a particular goal.
key performance indicator (KPI)	A metric that an organization tracks and measures, which generally drives which activities are the focus of organization.
leveraging	Investing with borrowed money, which can increase potential gains but also risks greater losses.
localization	Adapting a product to a region/culture/locale. This includes translation and adding content designed to appeal to local audiences.
minimum viable product (MVP)	A product, typically from a startup, with enough features to attract early-adopter customers and validate the product idea.
nonimmigrant visa	Visas for temporary residence in the United States, which do not lead to citizenship. These include H-1B, L-1, E-1, E-2, E-3, F-1, J-1, O-1, TN, and B-1 visas.

non-U.S. national Term for people who are not citizens of the United States, including both immigrants and expats.

preferred stock Securities that have priority over common stockholders in the event of liquidation. Generally, preferred stock has a fixed dividend, but no voting rights.

Program Electronic Review Management (PERM) The series of steps an employer must follow to prove that no U.S. citizen worker is available to fill the position and wages will not be driven down by hiring a foreign worker. The PERM enables employers to sponsor a non-U.S. national for a green card.

promissory note Signed document that contains a written promise to pay a stated sum to specified person or the bearer of the note at a set date or "on demand."

resident alien Term used by U.S. Internal Revenue Service (IRS) to describe non-U.S. citizens living in the United States and considered residents for tax purposes. To be considered a "resident alien," a person must be physically present in the United States for 31 days in a calendar year, or else for 183 days in the past three years.

sales agent Person or organization that sells products and services on behalf of other companies. Typically, sales agents represent multiple brands.

sales representative Person who works directly for a company to sell its products and services in a market. International companies that hire U.S.-based sales representatives need to establish a U.S. business entity.

sales and use taxes Sales tax applies to retail sales of certain tangible personal property and services. Use tax applies to certain products bought outside the state and used within that state.

serviceable addressable market (SAM) The segment of the total addressable market (TAM) targeted by your products and services that is within your geographical reach.

serviceable obtainable market (SOM) The portion of serviceable addressable market (SAM) that your company can capture.

scale To increase revenue at a much faster rate than the costs your company incurs.

scale-up Organizations with an established business model that are looking to dramatically increase their business and revenue.

Simple Agreement for Future Equity (SAFE) Agreement often used by entrepreneurs to raise money quickly to fund early-stage companies. Investors are given the right to receive equity on certain triggering events, such as sale of the company.

slotting fees Money demanded by grocery and other retail stores for adding a product to its warehouse and store shelves.

startup A company in the early stages of operations that is founded by one or more entrepreneurs with the goal of building profitable business.

transfer pricing The price at which related parties can transact with each other, such during the trade of supplies or finished products. The related parties can be a company and its subsidiaries, or divisions of the same company in different countries. This is also known as *transfer cost.*

total addressable market (TAM) Total potential revenue for a product or service if it has 100 percent market share in geographic region. This is also known as total available market.

unicorn Term used in the venture capital industry to describe a privately held startup company with a value of more than $1 billion.

venture capitalist (VC) Private investor or firm that provides capital to companies with high growth potential in exchange for an equity stake. This could be funding startup ventures or supporting small companies that want to expand but do not have access to equities markets.

About the Author

MATTHEW LEE SAWYER is an American business and marketing strategist, consultant, and author. For 25 years, Matthew worked in management roles and marketing agencies for several successful companies, including BIC USA, Campbell's Soup, Chinet division of Huhtamaki, Morgan Stanley, Pitney Bowes, and Snapple Beverages. Later, he worked for two digital technology startup companies. Currently, Matthew is the managing director of the strategy consulting firm Rocket Market Development and teaches graduate courses in business strategy and marketing communications at Columbia University and New York University.

Matthew received a Bachelor of Business Administration (BBA) from the University of Michigan in Ann Arbor and a Master of Business Administration (MBA) from New York University.

About the Author

Index